SAMURAI
CHESS

SAMURAI
CHESS

MASTERING STRATEGIC THINKING THROUGH THE MARTIAL ART OF THE MIND

MICHAEL J. GELB *and* RAYMOND KEENE

WALKER AND COMPANY
New York

First published in Great Britain by Aurum Press in 1997; published in the United States of America in 1998 by Walker Publishing Company, Inc.

Published simultaneously in Canada
by Thomas Allen & Son Canada, Limited, Markham, Ontario

Library of Congress Cataloging-in-Publication Data
Gelb, Michael J.
Samurai chess: mastering strategic thinking through the martial art
of the mind/Michael J. Gelb and Raymond Keene.
p.   cm.
Originally published: London: Aurum Press, 1997. With new index.
Includes bibliographical references (p.   ) and index.
ISBN 0-8027-1337-8. –ISBN 0-8027-7549-7 (pbk.)
1. Chess—Psychological aspects. I. Keene, Raymond D. II. Title.
GV1448.G45   1998
794.1–dc21   97-47512
CIP

Book design by Dede Cummings Designs

Printed in the United States of America
2 4 6 8 10 9 7 5 3 1

To my teacher and friend Clyde Takeguchi, Shihan

—M. G.

To the memory of Mikhail Botvinnik, who became World Champion in 1948, the year of my birth, and who first introduced me to the secrets of chess strategy.

—R. K.

Nature gave us the chessboard,
which we neither can nor will get out of;
Nature carved those pieces,
whose value, movement and ability gradually become familiar;
then it's up to us to make moves. . . .

—Goethe, *Schrift zur Naturwissenschaft*

When you attain the Way of strategy there will not be one thing you cannot see.

—Miyamoto Musashi, *A Book of Five Rings*

CONTENTS

PART I
SAMURAI CHESS—
THE CUTTING EDGE OF INTELLECTUAL CAPITAL

PART II
WHITE BELT CHESS

PART III
TRAINING FOR MENTAL COMBAT

PART IV
THE SEVEN SAMURAI PRINCIPLES

ACKNOWLEDGMENTS

The authors offer special thanks to HSH Prince Philipp von und zu Liechtenstein, sponsor of the LGT Academy, to Tony Buzan and Vanda North, Dean and Vice-Dean of the Academy, and to Muriel Nellis, our brilliant agent, and Jane Roberts, her associate. We also wish to thank Jackie Johnson, Chris Carey, and George Gibson of Walker and Company, and Christopher Pick. We are particularly and eternally grateful to Annette Keene and Nusa Maal Gelb for their love and support.

In particular, Michael Gelb would personally like to thank all his martial arts teachers, partners, and friends, especially: Kevin Bedgood, Dee Chen, Dr. Deng, Forrest Hainline, Nobou Iseri, Mitsunari Kanai, Ruth Kissane, Harvey Konigsberg, George Leonard, Mr. Ma, Greg O'Connor, Bill Plank, Zenko Okimura, Roger Paden, Wendy Palmer, Floyd Patterson, John Ramo, Carlos "Rocky" Rodriguez, Mitsugi Saotome, Jim Sorrentino, Rick Stickles, Pete Trimmer, Beth Ullman, Yoshimitsu Yamada, and all the instructors and students of Capital Aikikai and Aikido Shobukan Dojo. He is also grateful to his clients who apply the principles of Samurai Chess, particularly Jim D'Agostino, Ed

Bassett, Alex Cappello, Peter Cocoziello, marvelous Marv Damsma, Doug Durand, Gerry Kirk, and Delano Lewis, and to Audrey Ellzey and Julie Leinberger, his wonderful staff at High Performance Learning.

The authors and publishers are grateful for permission to quote from *A Book of Five Rings* (translated by Victor Harris) published by Allison and Busby, and to Bruce Lee, *Tao of Jeet Kune Do* (Ohara Publications, Inc., Santa Clarita, Calif., 1975) © Copyright 1975 by Linda Lee. Reprinted by permission of the publisher. They would also like to thank the following for their kind permission to reproduce the photographs and illustrations in this book: Archive Photos/*The Times* (London) (v, bottom); *A Book of Five Rings* (xv); Charles Sykes/Rex Features Ltd (11); Archive Photos/LDE (20); Tyrone Dukes/New York Times Co./Archive Photos and Archive Photos (21); Reuters/Pete Skingley Archive Photos (24); From *Sword of No Sword* by John Stevens, © 1984. Reprinted by arrangement with Shambala Publications, Inc., Boston (34); Bruce Lee, *Tao of Jeet Kune Do* (Ohara Publications, Inc., Santa Clarita, Calif., 1975) © Copyright 1975 by Linda Lee. Reprinted by permission of the publisher (40); IBM United Kingdom Ltd (127); Chris Harris/Times Newspapers Ltd (157). The diagrams on pages 168, 169, and 171 were drawn by Chapman Bounford & Associates. Photographs of Takeguchi (v) and Ueshiba (37) are from Michael Gelb's collection.

PREFACE

THE ORIGINS OF THIS BOOK

I first met Raymond Keene during a formal dinner held at Simpson's-in-the-Strand, the world-famous London restaurant, to celebrate the twenty-first anniversary of the publication of Tony Buzan's book *Use Your Head*. Raymond was charming, witty, warm, and remarkably erudite, and my wife, Nusa, commented that he seemed a cross between a classic English gentleman and a lovable teddy bear. The next time we met, I was sitting across the chessboard from him as one of twenty-eight players in a simultaneous display. He moved from board to board with a steely resolve that conjured up images of Rocky Marciano cutting off the ring and closing in for a knockout. The group included some highly rated chess players, but Raymond not only won all the games—he *crushed* everyone. Facing him over the chessboard was like attempting to attack my *aikido sensei* or trying to stop a *tsunami*. After the devastation was complete, the gentleman teddy bear returned; graciously, he went from board to board re-creating the game with each participant and showing each of us how we went wrong and what we might do differently next time. His patience and generosity seemed boundless as, fueled only by an occasional sip of Bollinger, he stayed up until four in the morning answering our questions, re-creating and commenting on classic games from the history of chess, and relating the development of chess strategy to the evolution of culture.

My next meeting with Raymond occurred when we were both invited to join the faculty of the Liechtenstein Global Trust Academy. This unique three-week residential leadership development program is conceived and deaned by Tony Buzan and sponsored by His Serene Highness, Prince Philipp von und zu Liechtenstein, LGT's chairman. Raymond was invited to teach chess, mind sports, and the history of genius and strategy, while I was asked to serve as Vice-Dean, teaching creative thinking, accelerated learning, leadership skills, and martial arts. For me, the highlight of the program was attending Raymond's class each evening. And I was delighted that each day the Grandmaster himself donned a traditional *gi* (martial arts uniform) and white belt to participate in my aikido classes. When we weren't teaching or attending each other's classes, we spent long hours discussing the nature of strategy in chess, martial arts, business, and life. As these conversations progressed, the book emerged. We hope you have as much fun reading it as we have had writing it.

—Michael Gelb

AUTHORS' NOTE

THE ESSENCE OF SAMURAI CHESS

In mid-seventeenth-century Japan Miyamoto Musashi, the invincible Samurai warrior, wrote *Go Rin No Sho, A Book of Five Rings*, a penetrating analysis of victorious Samurai strategy. For over three centuries this martial arts masterpiece remained a Japanese secret, but in 1974 it was discovered by the West. Almost overnight, the new translation sold more that 120,000 copies in hardback, catapulted to best-seller status in paperback, and drew lavish praise from leading newspapers around the world.

Time magazine wrote: "On Wall Street, when Musashi talks, people listen." The *New York Times* added that Musashi's strategy was "suddenly a hot issue on Wall Street." *Time Out* capped it all with: "If you have wondered how it is that the Japanese can cleave through Western business communities like a Samurai sword through butter, the answer lies with Musashi."

FROM ONE THING, KNOW TEN THOUSAND

Musashi's central message is one of "wider application," of "transferability." Achieving mastery in one discipline arms you with the weapon to transfer those skills to all other areas of life. Although on the surface Musashi's book is specifically a guide to Samurai swordsmanship, at deeper levels it provides a blueprint for strategy, decision, and action in the home, on the battlefield, in the corporate boardroom—in fact, wherever you choose to apply it.

Musashi summarized its essence thus, stating and restating his theme throughout the book: "From one thing, know ten thousand things. When you attain the Way of strategy there will not be one thing you cannot see. . . . If you know the Way broadly you will see it in everything."

THE MIND SPORTS METAPHOR

In spite of its undoubted brilliance, Musashi's book has two drawbacks for a modern audience. First, Musashi frequently expresses himself in a sometimes obscure and often impenetrable Zen terminology. Secondly, the late-twentieth-century reader will find it difficult, if not impossible, to participate at any meaningful level in Musashi's prime metaphor, that of Samurai swordsmanship, when with a real blade you face an opponent whom you must kill before he kills you. We are not likely to wield a Samurai sword in a life-or-death situation. Samurai swordsmanship will always remain beyond our personal experience.

Accordingly, this book turns to the easy-to-learn game of chess, already well established as an important thinking and business metaphor. It reinterprets and updates Musashi's martial arts message and extends it through a new dimension, a martial art of the mind.

In its various manifestations (Western, Japanese, and Chinese) chess is the world's most popular mind sport, with well over 400 million devotees. Chess is also at the cutting edge of the quest for artificial intelligence. World Champion Garry Kasparov regularly faces off in matches in New York and Philadelphia against IBM's Deep Blue supercomputer in which million-dollar prize funds are at stake.

VICTORY WITHOUT KILLING

Most important, though, chess offers the experience of real victory, without killing, and the parallel experience of real defeat, without having to die. Playing chess, you face pressure of time, you must assess risk accurately, and you must think globally and locally: In other words, it is all up to you. You truly win or you truly lose.

There are no accidental or chance results in chess. The ethos of entitlement and the syndrome of blaming others for setbacks are both alien to the game. Indeed, it is the qualities of personal enterprise and self-reliance that distinguish chess. The chess player should not blindly accept the pronouncements of authority. Thinking for yourself is what counts. At the chessboard, real situations beckon and, as Musashi would have put it, in mastering chess, you master in microcosm all forms of combat and strategy, for any application you may choose.

Miyamoto Musashi practicing fencing with two sticks, from a series of prints, Fidelity in Revenge, *by Kuniyoshi, c. 1848.*

PART I

SAMURAI CHESS– THE CUTTING EDGE OF INTELLECTUAL CAPITAL

1

INTRODUCTION

After reading *Samurai Chess*, you will know a great deal about martial arts, but you will not actually be trained for physical combat. However, you will be significantly better at chess, and you will learn an approach to winning based on martial arts' principles that will significantly improve your strength. And whether you are a novice or an experienced player, you will come to enjoy a unique metaphor for success in business and life.

How to Use This Book

To **complete beginners** (i.e., those who have never played the game) we offer in Part Two, "White Belt Chess," a comprehensive, step-by-step introduction to chess. As you learn the rules, objectives, basic strategy, and tactics you will also be guided to begin thinking like the greatest strategists of all time—the Samurai. When you complete this section you will have the opportunity to take your first White Belt chess exam. We are confident that you will succeed!

We advise **casual players** (those who play occasionally, usually with friends, but do not record their moves or use a chess clock) to review the basics of the game presented in Part Two and then take the White Belt test. Don't worry if you find it too easy—you will have ample opportunity to test yourself in Part Four, "The Seven Samurai Principles." If you study these principles carefully, and apply them consistently, you will crush other casual players.

We remind **serious players** of the old Japanese saying, "When you have completed 95 percent of your journey, you are halfway there." As you climb the mountain of chess the air gets thinner and progress can seem elusive. *Samurai Chess* offers advanced players an edge, an approach to strategy, and new ideas on achieving razor-sharp mental fitness that can add Elo ("rating"), points, and enjoyment. Our advice on personal fitness and diet, never before published in a chess manual, will help top players to reach and maintain their personal competitive peaks. Zen masters speak of the importance of cultivating "Beginner's Mind." So we recommend that at the least you should skim Part Two before moving on to the more advanced material. Pretend that you are learning the game anew. *Samurai Chess* aims to free you from the constrictions of old, unconscious habits of play and so liberate your full potential as a mental warrior.

If it were a game only, chess would never have survived the serious trials to which it has, during the long time of its existence, been often subjected. By some ardent enthusiasts chess has been elevated into a science or an art. It is neither; but its principal characteristic seems to be—what human nature mostly delights in—a fight. Not a fight, indeed, such as would tickle the nerves of coarser natures, where blood flows and the blows delivered leave their visible traces on the bodies of the combatants, but a fight in which the scientific, the artistic, the purely intellectual element holds undivided sway.

—Emanuel Lasker,
World Chess Champion 1894 to 1921

WHY PLAY CHESS?

Chess is open to everyone, regardless of age, gender or economic status, and offers many specific and profound benefits.

Developing memory power

International Grandmasters can play up to a hundred opponents simultaneously and remember all the moves from each game. They were not born with this skill—they developed it through intense practice and concentration. Memory is the cornerstone of intelligence and the database for creative thinking. All creative thinking is the result of new combinations of recalled ideas. As you learn chess openings and basic patterns of play you begin to flex and strengthen your memory muscles.

Slowing the aging process

According to Leonardo da Vinci, "Iron rusts from disuse, water that does not flow becomes stagnant, so it is with the human mind." Much of what passes for mental decline with age results from "disuse." Research has shown that individuals who regularly play mental sports are less susceptible to Alzheimer's and other diseases associated with advancing years. Chess keeps your mind agile, strong, and clear as you get older.

Aesthetics

Chess is beautiful. The artist Marcel Duchamp believed that "every chess player experiences a mixture of two aesthetic pleasures: firstly, the abstract image, linked with the poetic idea of writing; secondly the rational pleasure of ideographically implementing this image on the chessboard. Not all artists may be chess players, but all chess players are artists."

Chess is a sensual as well as a "purely mental" delight. A good chess set is a work of art. As you play and learn in this vibrant universe of black and white squares, you come to love the feel of the pieces in your hand, and to revel in the dramatic diagonal sweep of the bishop, the delightful leap of the knight, and the powerful thrust of the rook.

Self-knowledge and insight into others

For those given to reflection, chess offers a mirror to self-understanding. Can you follow through when you have made a plan? How do you hold up under pressure? Are you impatient? Are you mentally lazy? Can you manage time? Do you play to win or to draw? Does fear of making mistakes prevent you from trying something creative? Do you attend to details? Are you a gracious winner, a sore loser?

As well as teaching you about your own strengths and weaknesses, chess can develop your ability to understand others. To succeed at chess, you must learn to think like your opponent, even if your opponent's style of thinking is very different from your own.

Life is like a game of chess: we draw up a plan; this plan, however, is conditional on what—in chess, our opponent—in life, our fate—will choose to do.

—Arthur Schopenhauer,
Parerga and Paralipomena, 1851

Stronger decision-making and accountability

In many areas of life, one can get by with waffling, finger pointing, and obfuscation, but not on the chessboard. Chess is a game of decision making. The root of the word *decide* means "to kill the alternatives." In chess, you must decide on a move in a given time, make it, and be prepared to live with the consequences. As

World Champion Emanuel Lasker commented, "On the chessboard, lies and hypocrisy do not survive long."

Sharpening analytical and strategic thinking

Asked what use chess was, the German philosopher Gottfried Wilhelm Leibniz replied that it provided "practice in the ability to think and innovate. Wherever we have to make use of reason, we need an elaborate method to reach our goals. And moreover: a person's resourcefulness is most apparent when playing."

Innovation and "resourcefulness" are even more important today. The ability to analyze a problem, plan its solution, and then carry out that plan is life's most important skill. Chess hones this ability in a unique and dramatically effective fashion.

Improvement of . . . endeavor, the prevention of idleness, and the training of far-sighted, logical mental enjoyment.

—Jacobus de Cessolis, writing in about 1300 about the invention of chess. De Cessolis was a Dominican monk who employed chess allegories in his sermons

And one more thing, for many of the 400 million people around the world who play chess, there is one benefit of the game that reigns supreme: It's fun!

Arabian writings of the 10th century A.D. not only praised the beauty of chess, the authors of the period also recommended chess as an educational aid in the development of logical thinking. They also held the opinion that chess could lead to an insight into things to come, could enhance friendships, and also protect against loneliness. The Arabs became enthusiastic players and all classes of society were enchanted by the game. Even the Caliphs played and were very generous to the masters, the best of whom was As-Suli, showering them with gold and gifts. As-Suli's fame was so great that he was later credited with having invented the game. Almost 300 years later it was still considered a great honor for a master to be likened to As-Suli.

—Finkenzeller, Ziehr and Buhrer,
Chess: a Celebration of 2000 Years

APPLYING CHESS-BASED SKILLS

Ask any top headhunter what kind of person they seek to hire for senior management positions. They will tell you that, besides the basics of strong analytical and decision-making skills, they need people with superior strategic-thinking abilities who are willing to be accountable for their actions: people with insight into others, who can plan and act under pressure, especially in the face of uncertainty. There is no better way to develop these abilities than through chess and other mind sports.

A background in chess may prove better preparation for business success than even an MBA or a Ph.D. In 1990 Bankers Trust, a leading US financial institution, ran advertisements in *Chess Life*, the world's widest-read chess magazine, seeking talent for its trading division. The advertisements generated over 1,000 résumés; the bank interviewed a hundred respondents and hired five, two of them Grandmasters, the other three International Masters.

One of the gurus behind the program was international chess master Norman Weinstein, who became the bank's top foreign exchange trader, before moving on to Odyssey Partners. Weinstein attributes his success to his chess background. In an interview in 1994 with *Forbes* magazine, Weinstein emphasized:

> In chess, you learn to plan variations of play, to make a decision tree. One thing I find myself better in than most people is developing a strategy and implementing it. I'll say, "If he does this, we'll do that," whereas many very, very bright people will talk in generalities.

As an example Weinstein discussed his approach to analyzing the possible breakup of the European monetary system.

> To make a play on this involved shorting a number of currencies, which is very expensive to do. So I . . . did a poll of traders and economists, asked them to guess the probabilities of a breakup, and ran these through the risk-return analysis. The results made it clear that it would be profitable to keep on shorting the market, despite the day-to-day losses. It paid off in about one month.

He added that chess develops talent for rapidly calculating probabilities—spotting opportunities and balancing risks against rewards. At the same time it also cultivates willingness to stick to a strategy, even when it produces losing streaks in the short run, an essential trait for investment managers and business leaders. SKANDIA, the international finance giant, used a powerful chess theme throughout its 1995 report on value-creating processes and intellectual capital.

Michael Becker, a champion mental athlete and trader on the American Stock Exchange, told *Forbes* that chess is the ideal way to develop analytical ability. He recruits and trains traders and always looks for accomplished chess players. One of his most successful trainees is Ronald Henley, a Grandmaster who now runs his own firm. Becker says that traders with a background in mental sports consistently outperform their colleagues.

As part of an intensive three-week leadership training course, the top 250 managers of LGT, the international banking and investment company, all receive daily instruction in chess and other mental sports. Gerard Quirke, European Operations Director for LGT's asset management business, told Raymond Keene:

> We now have a thriving LGT International Chess Group, with people playing every day, even on electronic mail, with colleagues from all over the world. Learning to play chess as part of the course acted like aerobic exercise, but on the mind. It was like a personal fitness regime for the brain.

Notable Chess Players

Alexius Comnenus, the eleventh-century Byzantine emperor, was allegedly playing chess when he was surprised by a murderous conspiracy. Being a good chess player, he managed to escape! In real life the Aladdin of the fairy tale was a chess player, a lawyer from Samarkand in the court of Tamburlaine, the fourteenth-century conqueror of much of Asia. Tamburlaine himself loved to play chess; he named his son Shah Rukh, for he was moving a rook when the birth was announced. Goethe was an avid chess-player and believed that the game was essential to the cultivation of the intellect. Benjamin Franklin, another genius, was also an enthusiast—his *Morals of Chess*, published in 1786, was the first chess publication in America. Shakespeare and Einstein praised chess; Ivan the Terrible, Queen Elizabeth I, Catherine the Great, and Napoleon were all chess enthusiasts, while Lenin described chess as "the gymnasium of the mind."

Today top people in sport, science, politics, broadcasting and the media, medicine, business, and finance all sharpen their mental edges with chess.

Tony Buzan is a psychologist and writer, international TV presenter, and best-selling author on the brain. His books have been translated into fifteen languages and have sold 3 million copies. He regularly conducts business seminars in which he insists that chess is taught as a paradigm of strategic thinking skills.

Elaine Garzarelli, one of Wall Street's most celebrated and successful trend predictors, bases her analysis on economic indicators rather than on technical information supplied by individual companies. In 1995 and 1996 she successfully forecast most of the market's major moves. *Institutional Investor* named her Wall Street's top quantitative analyst for no less than eleven years in succession. She claims that her competitive instincts were fashioned as a child, when she fought her brother over the chessboard.

Legendary movie director Steven Spielberg likens filmmaking

to playing chess: "Directing is about seeing twenty moves ahead while you're working on the next five. I'm deciding whether to use my castle or my second bishop. How am I being threatened here? How can I advance?"

Lennox Lewis, the world heavyweight boxing champion, has repeatedly stated that he hones his strategic skills with chess. He has extolled the game's virtues on TV and has appeared on the front covers of chess magazines. He is a prime example of the new breed of sportsman that outthinks the opposition.

Sir Tim Rice has been a chess enthusiast since his early years. Celebrated as the lyricist for blockbuster musicals, including *Evita, Jesus Christ Superstar,* and *The Lion King,* he plowed all his chess expertise into the musical *Chess,* loosely based on the careers of Bobby Fischer and Soviet defector Viktor Korchnoi. For several years *Chess,* which opened in 1986, was one of the highlights of London theatrical life.

World heavyweight champion Lennox Lewis plans his ring strategy over the chessboard.

THE RAGE OF NEW YORK

It is a grave mistake to think that chess, the intellectual game of profound concentration and Trappist silence, is an antisocial game, or that its players are all drawn from intellectual and social elites. Throughout the world its appeal is deep-rooted, and it shows that intelligence—like a cultured foot or fist—is no respecter of conditioning or class. In New York's parks, games are played at lightning speed (only wimps need time to think), with resident hustlers pocketing an endless flow of bets. To chess traditionalists, this is startling enough. Even more significant, chess has proved itself a game, like football or boxing, that can lift poor kids out of the ghetto.

The Raging Rooks, a team from Adam Clayton Powell Junior School in Harlem, are an example. In April 1991, four students from this school in one of the most deprived areas in the whole of New York, wiped the board with teams from sixty other schools—some private and elite, and just about all of them better off than themselves—to win the U.S. Chess Federation's National Junior Championships. They had hardly been out of Harlem before. One of them had never even ridden in an elevator. Yet suddenly they had to get used to the full glare of the media as they became champions of the mind.

WOMEN AND CHESS

The world has become accustomed to brilliant results by the Hungarian prodigy Judit Polgar. But although an increasing number of female players are pushing to the fore, male chess players still form the great majority in top-level international competitions. Why should this be the case?

In Arabic times around A.D. 1000 many stories circulated concerning powerful female chess players. During the Renaissance in Europe, the playing of chess by women was a common theme in contemporary art. Even as late as the eighteenth century, the English artist Angelica Kaufmann, whose tondos adorn the foyer of London's Royal Academy, could depict herself playing chess as a symbol of the abstract notion of Composition. It was only during the late nineteenth and early twentieth centuries, when chess became accepted as a possible profession, that the role of female players receded into the background. Indeed, for most of the twentieth century, male and female players have been segregated into separate championships.

This is all now due to change, and probably quite swiftly. Unlike physical activities, mental sports such as chess present absolutely no barriers to competition of gender or physical strength. The time will doubtless—and soon—come when Judit or one of her followers will be competing in her own right for the absolute championship of the world.

Nigel Short has freely admitted that his greatest embarrassment came when he lost to the Georgian Maya Chiburdanidze. One of Argentina's top chess players is Claudia Amura. Two of Britain's champion players, John Nunn and James Plaskett, have both recently been beaten not just by teenagers, but by teenage girls. Nobody likes to be beaten. Men especially do not like to be beaten by women. But they will have to get used to it, for although there have been a number of good women players this century, in the 1990s there has been a rush of talent around the world. Among those at the top of the ratings are Alisa Maric from Yugoslavia, Nana Ioseliani from Georgia, Pia Cramling from Sweden, teenager Hoanng Trang from Vietnam, and Xie Jun, the former Women's World Champion, from China.

The Polgar sisters

According to Cathy Forbes, the former British Women's Champion, one of the reasons women are on a roll is the startling success of the Hungarian Polgar sisters. These young women, raised to be masters of the game by their dedicated and ambitious father Laszlo, have all turned out to be extraordinarily successful. "Their achievement has inspired a generation of women and girls," says Forbes, who has written a book, *The Polgar Sisters,* about the family. "The growth in the last seven years has been amazing. There used to be just a handful of good women chess players. Now they're all very good."

To Forbes, the Polgar experiment shows exactly what she herself has long believed—that excellence in chess can be taught. Girls are not born mentally less well equipped than boys; it is nurture, not nature, that makes the difference.

2

CHESS AND THE EVOLUTION OF CULTURE

THE FIRST BOARD GAMES

Games have been played since the dawn of civilization some ten thousand years ago. The earliest writings regularly refer to games similar in concept to tic-tac-toe. As a society progressed, so did the complexity of its games.

Irving Finkel of the Western Asiatic Antiquities Department at the British Museum is an expert on the earliest board games:

There are different schools of thought on the origins of games. Some people think that they came out of divination practice. The apparatus for divination—dice and ritual boards—may have later been used for entertainment. Others think it was the other way around. In 1923, when Sir Leonard Woolley excavated the royal graves at Ur in Mesopotamia, he discovered five sets of a game played around 3000 to 2600 B.C. This game has become known as the Royal Game of Ur and it is usually quoted as the earliest known. It was a ferocious gambling game. Some insight as to how it was played can be gleaned from a detailed inscription within the tombs. Around this time there was a belief that the deceased must play the game with one of the underworld deities to guarantee safe passage into the afterlife. The inscription concentrates on betting strategy—presumably advice to the dead king from the game's contemporary experts.

Play was similar to modern ludo or backgammon, with pieces being moved into, along, and off the board according to the throw of pyramid-shaped dice. A fine example is on exhibit at the Museum.

According to Dr. Finkel, more recent archaeological discoveries in Palestine and Jordan may make the Royal Game of Ur a relative newcomer. Game boards have been found that can be dated back to Neolithic times, some 4000 years before the Royal Game of Ur. "At that time," he says, "we had large urban conglomerations of people with controlled livestock, domesticated plants and animals. There was specialization of labor. And there was obviously, in daily life, room for amusements."

In 1989, Gary Rollefson of San Diego State University discovered a stone game board at Ain Ghazal, Jordan. This and other similar discoveries have been dated to between 7000 and 6000 B.C. Though we cannot be certain of their purpose, there is strong evidence to suggest they are game boards. Their layout is very similar to the traditional seed-sowing game of mancala, which is popular to this day across Africa. If these tablets were indeed used for recreation, Middle Eastern civilizations had developed board-type games before they could write or even make pottery.

HOW CHESS BEGAN

The ancient ancestor of chess was an Arabic game called *shatranj*. It was popular in Baghdad by the eighth century A.D., but its origins can be traced back as far as 350 B.C. *Shatranj* was a slow-moving game in which the queen and bishop had much less freedom of movement than their modern counterparts; nonetheless it was recognizably chess.

The ancestry of *shatranj* spanned two continents and—appropriately for a war game—was a by-product of a military campaign. The bloodline may be traced back more than 2000 years to ancient Greece. In his *Politics,* Aristotle mentions a group of classical board games called *petteia.* These were battle games that demanded skill, logic, and reason, not simply the fortuitous throw of a die. In the *Republic,* Plato compares victims of Socrates' debating skill with "weak petteia players . . . cornered and rendered unable to move." In about 330 B.C. Alexander the Great invaded Persia and marched on toward Asia Minor and India. Along the way he founded Hellenic colonies in which the Greeks continued their passion for *petteia.* At the same time India had a battle game of its own. It shared its Sanskrit name, *chaturanga,* meaning "four divisions," with the Indian army. The divisions in question were elephants, chariots, cavalry, and infantry, all mobilized in the game by throws of dice.

It did not take long for *chaturanga,* the Indian war game of chance, to meet and marry *petteia,* the Greek game of reason. The effect of *petteia* on *chaturanga* was to eliminate the dice, and from this collision of cultures, chess—Greek thought expressed in Indian language—was born. The Muslim Arabs adopted it, and translated the Indian *chaturanga* into the Arabic *shatranj.*

Via the squares on a chessboard, the Indians explain the movement of time and the age, the higher influences which control the world and the ties which link chess with the human soul.

—The Arabian historian Al-Masudi, writing in A.D. 947

THE RENAISSANCE: EXPANSION OF POSSIBILITY

Not until about 1470 did chess begin its transformation from the slow Islamic form to the rapid-fire game we know today. Castling was introduced at this time, pawns gained the privilege of advancing two squares on their initial move, and the queen switched from being a waddling cripple (the Arabic vizier, allowed to move only one square at a time) to the most powerful piece on the board.

Recorded games of the time show all the exuberant naïveté of excited novices—the queen pursuing joyous adventures all over the board, giving check regardless of whether or not it offered the player any advantage. As chess is a game that symbolizes warfare, it is reasonable to suppose that the increased firepower of the queen reflected the introduction of field artillery in the late fifteenth century.

The sudden advance of chess as a whole must also have been a product of the Renaissance. An increasingly urgent perception of distance, space, and perspective distinguished human intellectual development. Parallel developments included the innovatory use of siege artillery to batter down the walls of Constantinople in 1453, scientific advances such as the telescope and the microscope, and the application of perspective in art.

The next country to exert decisive influence was Spain. After 1492 Spain rapidly became the dominant force in world communication, and the new form of chess spread across the world through her explorations and conquests. The *conquistadores* were keen players of a game that mirrored their combative lifestyle, and they taught it to the defeated Inca and Aztec kings in the New World.

THE MODERN GAME

The modern era of chess began with Wilhelm Steinitz, who became the first of thirteen World Champions in 1886. Every subsequent World Champion has pushed forward the boundaries of chess knowledge, science, and art, each in his own way reflecting the intellectual ethos of his day.

Steinitz was a contemporary of Darwin and Marx, who proposed rigid theories to elucidate the evolution of species and the nature of society and government. Like them, Steinitz tried to impose an ironclad theory on chess. In his case, it was the insistence that no attack could be successful unless a prior strategic advantage had been achieved. This contrasted strongly with previous practitioners of chess, who had not been averse to launching haphazard attacks, whatever the situation on the board.

Emanuel Lasker was World Champion in the early twentieth century. He was a philosopher who developed an entire intellectual program based on the struggle. He relied not on "theory," but on what worked against specific opponents. Good defenders were lured into unsound attacks, while avid attackers regularly found themselves exposed to Lasker's own mercilessly aggressive fire power.

In his foreword to Lasker's biography, none other than Albert Einstein paid tribute to Lasker's independence of thought:

Emanuel Lasker was undoubtedly one of the most interesting people I came to know in my later life. Few, indeed, can have combined such a unique independence of personality with so eager an interest in all the great problems of mankind. I met Emanuel Lasker in the house of a mutual friend and I came to know him well during the many walks we took together discussing ideas on a variety of subjects. It was a somewhat unilateral discussion in which, almost invariably, I was in the position of listener, for it seemed to be the natural thing for this eminently creative man to generate his own ideas, rather than adjust himself to those of someone else.

Milko Bobotsov and Tigran Petrosian

José Raoul Capablanca, the third Champion, mirrored the rise of the transatlantic New World, while the exiled Russian aristocrat Alexander Alekhine had a turbulent style based on revolutionary tactics, parallel with that of Dada and Surrealism in art and reflecting the contemporary political turmoil in Europe.

After World War II the USSR began to dominate world chess. The dynasty was founded with Mikhail Botvinnik's World Championship victory. Alekhine had died in 1946, and after a two-year interregnum Botvinnik took the title in 1948. Since then, with the single exception of Bobby Fischer, every World Champion has been from the former Soviet Union.

SOVIET AND RUSSIAN CHESS

Why was the Soviet Union, and subsequently Russia, so overwhelmingly successful at chess? From 1948 to 1972 the USSR

Bobby Fischer

Boris Spassky

WORLD CHESS CHAMPIONS

1886–94	Wilhelm Steinitz	Austria
1894–1921	Emanuel Lasker	Germany
1921–27	José Raoul Capablanca	Cuba
1927–35	Alexander Alekhine	Russia
1935–37	Max Euwe	Netherlands
1937–46	Alexander Alekhine	Russia
1948–57	Mikhail Botvinnik	USSR
1957–58	Vassily Smyslov	USSR
1958–60	Mikhail Botvinnik	USSR
1960–61	Mikhail Tal	USSR
1961–63	Mikhail Botvinnik	USSR
1963–69	Tigran Petrosian	USSR
1969–72	Boris Spassky	USSR
1972–75	Bobby Fischer	USA
1975–85	Anatoly Karpov	USSR
1985–	Garry Kasparov	USSR/Russia

dominated the World Championship, and thereafter still provided the vast majority of the world's elite Grandmasters. This has much to do with the gigantic material resources that the USSR plowed into achieving victory in virtually every international sport. In the collective mind of the Soviet regime, chess was not merely a sport; it also conferred intellectual respectability. Hence the game was worth substantial financial investment, in order to seize the World Championship and, by systematic nurturing of young players, consolidate and retain it.

There is a deeper reason. The Soviet state was notable for its lack of opportunity for free thought. Any book, article, pamphlet, idea, piece of music, or even poem might be considered ideologically unsound. The consequence for the writer, composer, or thinker who offended state orthodoxy ranged from ostracism to imprisonment in Arctic Circle labor camps and the ultimate sanction: summary execution.

In 1987, Joseph Brodsky, the dissident Soviet writer, was awarded the Nobel Prize for Literature. Earlier he had written: "Evil, especially political evil, is always a bad stylist." For expressing such sentiments he was sentenced to five years in a prison camp in Siberia. Brodsky also argued that "the surest defense against evil is extreme individualism and originality of thinking."

Here lies the true reason, aside from any state sponsorship, for the extraordinary popularity of chess in Soviet Russia. Chess offers a wide field for individual thought, in which the state has no right to interfere. Even in music, the top Soviet composer, Dimitri Shostakovich, was ridiculed by that well-known music critic Joseph Stalin, and lived in constant fear of arrest and deportation to a labor camp. Playing chess allowed Russians to free their minds from the shackles of state dogma. Not even a Soviet commissar would have dared to utter the words "Comrade, that move is ideologically unsound." In chess the sole criterion is whether the move is good or bad, whether it wins or loses. By playing chess, ordinary Russians reconquered for themselves a measure of personal liberty in their everyday lives, over which the state had no control. In chess they could pursue freedom and self-determination.

Children need to be encouraged to think rather than to follow blindly. Not thinking for themselves leads to horrendous consequences. The nation is engaged in a process of reduction of values and principles. Thinking almost seems to be out of the equation.

—Frances Lawrence, widow of London headmaster Philip Lawrence stabbed to death by a 16-year-old gang member outside his school in December 1995. Mrs. Lawrence was launching her manifesto for nationwide moral revival. (From *The Times*, October 19, 1996)

In 1988, Professor Paul Kennedy published his book *The Rise and Fall of the Great Powers*, in which he argued that over-reliance on military strength and state security creates an imbalance with economic viability and can lead to the collapse of even the seemingly most impressive nation or empire. This was widely, but wrongly, interpreted as a dire prediction of the future of the USA. Kennedy's book far more accurately prophesied the imminent demise of the USSR. Indeed, within a further four years the USSR, as it had been constituted since the Revolution of 1917, no longer existed. A critical factor in the dissolution of the Soviet Union and the fall of its communist masters was the regime's dependence on restricting information and ideas. This was at the precise moment when the economies of the western world, and many in Asia, were on the brink of an information explosion, driven by new information-based technologies and reliant to an unprecedented degree on intellectual capital.

This message became apparent during the 1986 World Chess Championship between Garry Kasparov and Anatoly Karpov. The match was held in two equal halves, twelve games in London (organized by Raymond Keene), twelve in Leningrad, as St. Petersburg was then still known. As a standard facility for the International Press Corps, within five minutes of the end of each game the London logistics team printed a complete record of the moves and the times taken by each player, together with key comments

Garry Kasparov and Anatoly Karpov

by Grandmasters and printed diagrams of important situations in the game. Not only was this blitz report instantly available, it was also faxed to interested journalists around the world within a further five minutes.

In Leningrad, the contrast could not have been more marked. Three elderly babushkas typed up the moves as the game progressed. However, there was no photocopier at the Championship site in the Hotel Leningrad. The match Director, Secretary, and Press Chief had to sign a document in triplicate allowing the press assistant to take a cab to Communist Party Headquarters several miles away, the location of the only official photocopier in the city. Only on the press assistant's return after about forty-five minutes could the assembled international press corps discover what the official moves had been. It was obvious that for the USSR the game would soon be over.

CHESS AND ISLAM

Although totalitarian states, such as the USSR, could not dictate which chess moves to make, some particularly oppressive regimes have tried to solve the problem of free thought by banning chess completely. The news in October 1996 that the new Taleban regime in Afghanistan had banned the playing of chess should not surprise students of the game's checkered career under Islamic law. In the Islamic world over the past 1000 years or so, chess has from time to time been banned, and then the prohibition has been lifted again. When the Ayatollahs came to power in Iran, one of their first acts was to ban chess; the prohibition has now been relaxed and chess is permitted once again.

This periodically hostile attitude toward chess is curious, given that chess first flourished in the Baghdad Caliphate over 1000 years ago and that Harun al-Rashid, the Abbasid Caliph of Islam from A.D. 786 to A.D. 809, was known to be a chess player. The problem derives from a verse of the Koran that reads: "O true believers, surely wine and lots and images and divining-arrows are an abomination of the works of Satan, therefore avoid ye them that ye may prosper." Although chess is not specifically proscribed in the Koran, some Muslim lawyers in about A.D. 800 extended the condemnation of lots or dice and images to chess and chess players.

Ash-Shafii, the ninth-century Arab jurist, put forward counter-arguments, claiming that chess was an image of war and that the game could be played, not just for a stake or for pure recreation, but as a mental exercise for the solution of military tactics. This view has tended to prevail, not least because the Caliphs themselves were often avid chess players, and during the late ninth and early tenth centuries in Baghdad, kept a court retinue of aliyat, Grandmasters, who regularly conducted competitions for their amusement. Tradition states that the oldest chess problem on record was composed in 840 by the Caliph Mutasim Billah, third son and successor of Harun al-Rashid.

You can play chess anywhere. You can play by post, by fax, by telephone. You can play with home-made or improvised pieces. You can play an unseen opponent in jail—or you yourself can play from jail. If you are a Grandmaster you might even occasionally manage without a board at all, playing all the moves inside your head. Yet chess is not an exclusively private, indoor game. In European cities—in squares and parks, even in swimming pools—there is a long and lively tradition of outdoor chess, with crowds gathering to offer the protagonists the benefit of their (usually contradictory) advice. In the USA, not surprisingly, outdoor chess is rather different and is played at lightning speed—so high is the standard that even professional Grandmasters come along to practice their blitz games.

A NEW RENAISSANCE

The Soviet empire is no more, but the information revolution has accelerated and the value of intellectual capital continues to appreciate. Playing chess remains one of the most powerful methods of cultivating a disciplined, free, and powerful intellect.

Once perceived as a contest for geeks and nerds with nothing better to do, chess has changed its image. Chess Grandmasters are increasingly viewed as high-level mental athletes, commanding the world stage along with multimillion-dollar purses. Since 1972, when the mercurial American genius Bobby Fischer wrested the World Championship from Boris Spassky in Reykjavik, chess and its most prominent personalities have become international superstars.

Before he appeared, there was a thrill in the air, hard rock blaring from big speakers, people nudging one another, whispering "Kasparov." The champion entered, his arm in the air with a self-conscious smile that spurred a wave of cheering and applause. A couple of girls whispered "It's him." Everyone crowded around the tables of the players, creeping over shoulders to get a glimpse of his moves. We're talking about chess here, not Bruce Springsteen.

—U.S. chess writer Fred Waitzkin, reporting Kasparov's entrance to a simultaneous chess display in France in 1990

The increased prize fund for major contests reflects how much interest in chess has grown. In 1969 the World Chess Championship match was worth about 3,000 rubles (less than $3,000) to the winner. In 1990 Kasparov and Karpov contested a purse of $2 million. In 1993, for the Kasparov–Short contest, total investment in the match was nearly $10 million. Chess champions are now global brain stars.

I know of no spectacle on earth that can keep thousands of spectators enthralled for five hours. Utterly immobile and deep in thought, the players sit facing each other like the hieratic actors in a Japanese Kabuki production.

—Fernando Arrabal, the Spanish dramatist and chess writer, on the 1985 Moscow Championship

The correlation between success at chess and top-flight academic performance in the British school system is staggering. The same schools appear at the head of the list of top-scoring schools at A-level (the examinations taken at age eighteen) and are the most successful in the British Schools Chess Championship, supported by *The Times*. In some high-achieving independent schools in the U.K., chess is increasingly being seen as a core element of the curriculum designed to equip children to compete successfully in the global marketplace. By contrast, the U.K. government's National Curriculum, which all state-funded schools must follow, officially ignores chess, and indeed all mind sports. The only chance that the vast majority of the nation's children have to learn chess in school is if an enthusiastic teacher is prepared to give up free time to running a chess club. Yet it is increasingly acknowledged that chess and mind sports must become an essential aspect of training for the knowledge workers of the twenty-first century.

Bjorn Wolrath, president and CEO of SKANDIA, took a perceptive look forward in *Intellectual Capital: Value-Creating Processes*, his company's chess-themed supplement to its 1995 annual report.

> The future is in creating new work methods, competencies and value-creating processes, not just in following the beaten path. Future and knowledge-oriented leadership . . . must embrace a broader view and take into account more than the purely financial dimensions, namely, the hidden values in the balance sheet— employees' competence, computer systems, work processes, trademarks, customer lists and so on—are obtaining increasing importance in assessing the value of a company. This is intellectual capital—a combination of human and structural capital.

3

THE SAMURAI TRADITION AND MODERN MARTIAL ARTS

Chess is a sport, a violent sport. . . . If it's anything at all, then it's a fight.

—The painter Marcel Duchamp,
quoted in *Marcel Duchamp Plays and Wins*
by Yves Arman

Like chess, the martial arts have evolved over thousands of years. Fear of death has a unique way of concentrating the mind and martial strategy has developed accordingly. As we learn more about the martial arts we are continually amazed at the myriad sophisticated and diabolically clever methods people have created to protect themselves and inconvenience others. This phenomenal strategic databank can be applied for good or evil, and we aim to use it for good: specifically, to help you to improve your chess game and generally to hone your strategic skills in business and in life.

We draw our approach to strategy from many sources. Our strongest influence comes from the Samurai tradition of Japan, its greatest masters and modern pioneers: supreme swordsmen Miyamoto Musashi and Yamaoku Tesshu, judo founder Jigoro Kano, karate giant Gichin Funakoshi, and Morihei Ueshiba, the creator of aikido. While we recognize our debt to Japanese *budo* (the tradition of cultivating martial prowess, mental and spiritual development, and social responsibility), we must also acknowledge that we have been strongly influenced by two Chinese geniuses, one ancient, one modern. Sun Tzu, a Chinese general who lived 2,500 years ago, wrote a masterpiece of strategy titled *The Art of War*, which profoundly influenced the evolution of martial thought in Japan. Like Musashi's *A Book of Five Rings*, *The Art of War* has become an essential guidebook for military and business leaders everywhere. Bruce Lee (1949–73), known in the West primarily for his action movies, was a transcendentally magnificent martial artist and philosopher of strategy. His manual, the *Tao of Jeet Kune Do (The Way of the Intercepting Fist)*, represents a synthesis of the best of martial strategy and tactics from all traditions.

THE SAMURAI WARRIORS

The Samurai of Japan were the most remarkable warriors history has known. In western culture the closest parallel to the Samurai tradition is the code of the feudal chivalric knights. Like the Samurai, these legendary warriors were bound by duty, honor and loyalty to a lord. Both systems emphasized sophisticated ethics and high ideals allied with potent training methods and technologies for death and destruction. The unique Japanese combination of an isolated, island culture and prolonged civil wars allowed the incubation and evolution of the most refined and formidable warrior class ever. Feudal knights were willing to die for their lords; Samurai relished death. Knights carried large broadswords into battle; Samurai carried *katana*, the sharpest and most perfect blade ever constructed. A captured knight would bravely face punishment, but with the knowledge that he would probably be ransomed; a

Samurai would commit *seppuku*—kill himself by ripping out his own belly with a knife—rather than be captured.

The Samurai class emerged from the warrior clans, particularly the Minamoto and Taira, who struggled for control of Japan in the eleventh and twelfth centuries. The great general Yoritomi Minamoto eventually defeated the Taira in the Gempei Wars of 1181 to 1185. (Legends born during the Gempei Wars form many of the themes of Japanese literature and drama—*kabuki* and *noh*.) As he consolidated and administered his territory, Yoritomi established his headquarters in Kamakura. In 1192 the emperor granted him the title *Sei-i tai shogun*—"Barbarian Suppressing Generalissimo." According to Professor Richard Storry, author of *The Way of the Samurai*, "By the time the Gempei War had ended with the annihilation of the Taira . . . the distinctive ethos of the Samurai was firmly accepted on all sides."

This ethos, and the strategic concepts that accompanied it, continued to evolve over the centuries. Describing the development of the Samurai's amazingly effective and sophisticated approach to strategy, aikido *shihan* (professor or Grandmaster) Mitsugi Saotome comments, "Hundreds of thousands of warriors died in a continuing martial contest of natural selection. It is an evolution etched in blood."

Although Shintoism and Confucianism formed an aesthetic and ethical backdrop for the development of Samurai culture, the most significant element is the influence of Zen. Although Zen reached Japan by way of China in the seventh century, it flourished only after Minamoto's successors adopted its austere, highly effective methods for stilling the mind and strengthening the will.

The focus and extraordinary concentration the Samurai developed through the practice of Zen are often romanticized. The initial idea was to create a perfect warrior, ready to kill or die at any moment without the slightest hesitation. Central to the practice of Zen is the realization of *satori*, or Enlightenment. As Zen was married with warrior practice, rare individuals achieved martial *satori*, a state of combat mastery yielding indomitability. These enlightened martial Grandmasters founded various *ryu*, schools of combat strategy and technique that passed their wisdom from generation to generation. Although the sword remained the focus of martial practice, different *ryu* specialized in spear, staff, knife, and ingenious forms of hand-to-hand combat. During the rare periods of peace, the *ryu* continued to train, emphasizing the building of character and spiritual clarity.

Following many generations of internecine conflict, in 1603 Ieyasu, the first Tokugawa *shogun* and a descendant of the Minamoto clan, established an effective administration from Tokyo. The reign of the Tokugawa lasted more than 250 years, during which Japan closed itself from the outside world, and the Samurai code was further refined and formalized as *Bushido*—"The Way of the Warrior." In 1853 Commodore Perry's "Black Ships" appeared off the Japanese coast. The reopening of the islands and the end of the shogunate were now inevitable—the western barbarians could no longer be suppressed. In 1869 the Meiji Emperor reclaimed complete control of Japan for the imperial family and the stage was set for the birth of the modern Japanese nation.

The Samurai spirit survived, even though the wearing of the sword in public was forbidden in 1876 and the helmet, armor, war fans, and *kubibukoro* (a bag used to carry the head of a slain enemy) were soon to be seen only in museums, and later in films. Throughout the twentieth century Samurai strategy has been the dominant influence in Japanese military and business endeavors. Many of the leaders of twentieth-century Japan were nurtured in the *dojos* ("a place for training in the way") of the *ryu*. Although watered down, training in traditional martial arts remains a part of the basic Japanese school curriculum to this day.

The Modern Martial Arts

Kendo, judo, karate, and aikido—the martial arts that have evolved during approximately the last century—have also influenced our approach to Samurai chess. We offer here a brief introduction to the techniques and mental strategies they encourage.

Kendo

Kendo—"way of the sword"—remains very popular in Japan. Competitors wear helmets and body armor to protect themselves from their opponents' strikes with a *shinai*, a bamboo sword. Less popular but perhaps more elegant are the *ryu* that specialize in the "live sword." Some of these schools emphasize the perfect drawing and resheathing of the *katana*, while others actually move through ritualized forms of combat, razor-sharp blades passing within millimeters of pulsing veins.

The sword remains the dominant icon of Japan, and swordmasters are still revered as almost divine. From all the legendary swordmasters two stand out, Miyamoto Musashi and Yamaoku Tesshu. Although his life is shrouded in legend, we do know that Musashi, known in Japan as *Kensei* ("The Sword Saint"), was born in 1584. Musashi was a *ronin*, a Samurai without a lord, who fought in many battles both for and against Ieyasu, the first Tokugawa *shogun*. He is also said to have cut down more than sixty men in duels. Once proved invincible, Musashi exchanged his blade for brush and pen. An intellectual *ronin*, Musashi had a truly independent mind; he ignored traditional teachings and aimed to penetrate reality, using personal experience as his teacher. Attaining enlightenment, he retired to a cave in 1645 to record his philosophy. The result is perhaps the most extraordinary guide to strategy ever conceived, *Go Rin No Sho* (*A Book of Five Rings*). More than a thesis on sword fighting and battle strategy, *A Book of Five Rings* is designed "for any situation where plans and tactics are used." It has become required reading in corporate boardrooms and military schools worldwide.

Much more is known of Yamaoku Tesshu, who was born into a Samurai family in Tokyo on June 10, 1836. Tesshu's parents raised him to love classical learning, especially calligraphy and poetry, and the martial arts, sending him for special training in

Zen to cultivate the quality of *fudo-shin*, "imperturbable mind." His instruction in swordsmanship began when he was nine under the guidance of Inoue Kiyotora, master of the Ono-ha Itto *ryu*. A prodigy, Tesshu defeated thousands of opponents and terrorized kendo halls throughout the land. At twenty-eight, however, he met his nemesis in Asari Gimei, a swordmaster of the Nakanishi-ha Itto *ryu*. As tradition dictated, Tesshu promptly enrolled as a student of the victorious Asari. Training passionately and meditating daily on the *koans* (Zen puzzles based on paradox) his teacher offered, he attained enlightenment on March 30, 1880. He wrote:

> For years I forged my spirit through the
> study of swordsmanship,
> Confronting every challenge steadfastly.
> The Walls surrounding me suddenly crumbled;
> Like pure dew reflecting the world in crystal clarity, total
> awakening has now come.

Yamaoku Tesshu

Tesshu founded the Itto Shoden Muto *ryu* ("The Sword of No-Sword School"), which became renowned for highly intense training and ultrasophisticated strategy. The phrase "Sword of No-Sword" is a *koan*, and suggests that the true swordsman is so unified with his weapon that he treats it not as a separate entity but as an extension of himself. Tesshu's strategic brilliance was also apparent in his remarkable role as a diplomat—he played a key part in the peaceful transfer of power from the Tokugawa Shogunate to the Emperor. Mastery of the arts of calligraphy and poetry complemented his martial and strategic genius. Tesshu's life and work are summed up in his personal motto, which he inscribed on many of the thousands of works of calligraphy that he left behind: "When the spirit is unified it is amazing what can be accomplished!"

Judo

Jigoro Kano (1859–1938), the founder of judo ("the gentle way"), was a visionary who set the stage for twentieth-century martial arts. A classical scholar, linguist, and ethicist, Kano was above all else an educator. After gaining a *menkyo kaiden* (master teacher certificate) in Kito-ryu ju-jitsu at the age of twenty-four (ju-jitsu is an ancient and highly effective form of hand-to-hand combat that emphasizes throws, joint locks, grappling, choke holds, pressure points, and foot sweeps), Kano organized and codified the diverse ju-jitsu techniques into a rational, accessible system. He developed the formalized grading procedures and belt-ranking system now used by many other martial arts. Kano believed that the martial arts are a path to social education and character development. He pioneered the use of the term *do* ("path" or "road") in place of *jitsu* ("fighting method"). Kano's basic tenets were "creating mutual benefit for oneself and others" and "understanding the rational, efficient use of energy," manifested by the fundamental principle of Judo strategy: "If pushed, pull, if pulled, push."

Karate-do

Karate-do ("the way of the empty hand") is a devastatingly powerful martial art, characterized by lightning-fast punches and kicks. Its origins go back at least five hundred years to the Ryukyu Islands of Okinawa. After Sho Hashi, the Chuzan warlord, had unified Ryukyu's three warring provinces, he banned all weapons. The people responded by cultivating ingenious techniques for killing an opponent with a single strike of a bare hand or foot. (The islanders had long traded with Fukien Province in China, home of Kenpo, the Chinese boxing art, which is the likely ancestor of karate.)

Although karate has many different *ryu* and many legendary masters, Gichin Funakoshi (1868–1958), born a Samurai at the beginning of the Meiji restoration, is generally considered to be the father of the modern art. Like Kano, Funakoshi was primarily an educator. As a young man in Okinawa, he worked by day as a schoolteacher, then rushed to the home of his *sensei* ("respected teacher"—literally "one who was born before") to train until the early hours. He trained intensively for most of his life, and served his art as a humble, dedicated ambassador. He played a crucial role in developing the strategy, tactics, technique, and philosophy of karate and also in introducing it to the rest of the world.

Aikido

Aikido ("the way of harmonious spirit") was founded by Morihei Ueshiba (1883–1969). According to Professor John Stevens, who has written studies of Ueshiba and Tesshu, Ueshiba was "undoubtedly the greatest martial artist who ever lived." Of Samurai lineage, Ueshiba studied the martial ways with phenomenal fervor. He was strongly influenced by the traditions of sumo (wrestling), hozoin *ryu* (spear-fighting), yagyu *ryu* (sword), and especially daito *ryu* (ju-jitsu). Despite his diminutive frame (he was

Morihei Ueshiba

4 feet 11 inches tall), Ueshiba possessed almost superhuman strength; witnesses testify to his ability to uproot tree stumps with his bare hands! Ueshiba's physical strength and technical prowess were exceeded only by his spiritual intensity and depth of insight. The synthesis of these powers enabled him to fell would-be attackers with a shout (*kiai*) or glance.

Aikido *shihan* Mitsugi Saotome, one of the great martial artists alive today, recounts his experience of attacking Ueshiba during a demonstration:

> I attacked him with all my power; my only thought was to strike him down. The walls of the *dojo* shook as his *kiai* shattered the air and my entire body was imprisoned by the shock . . . the violent winds of a typhoon lashed my body. The force of his gravity sucked me deep into the vacuum of a black hole from which there was no escape. Deep within my core a bomb exploded and the whole universe expanded. There was nothing but light, blinding searing

light and energy . . . my mind and spirit were illuminated. . . . Then, I was unconscious.

When Saotome asked Ueshiba to explain what had happened, he replied, "I am empty. . . . My power is not my power. This is the universal power. Saotome, you attack a typhoon, a hurricane, a tornado. You are punching air, the clouds, a mountain. What do you feel when you strike the sun?"

When Jigoro Kano witnessed Ueshiba in action in 1930 he exclaimed, "This is the true judo." Inspired by Ueshiba's remarkable refinement of his own principles, Kano sent many of his senior students to train in aikido and to learn a new tenet: "If pulled, enter. If pushed, turn." Aikido strategy centers on applying elegant circular and spiral movements to "blend with" and "lead" the energy of an attack.

THE SAMURAI CHESS RANKING SYSTEM

In the martial arts, students master set techniques, known as *kata*, and test themselves in competition. As they improve, meeting the specific criteria of their art, they become eligible to test for rank. Judo's Jigoro Kano pioneered the modern *kyu/dan* belt system of signifying rank. Although the different arts interpret the belt systems in various ways, a general guideline for respectable schools is as follows. (Steer well clear of the many commercialized, bastardized "teenage-mutant-ninja-turtle *dojos*" who give out striped, plaid, and multicolored belts-of-the-month to students who hand over the necessary cash.)

> **Beginners** wear white belts (6th and 5th *kyu*)
> **Advanced beginners** wear green belts (4th and 3rd *kyu*)
> **Intermediate players** wear brown belts (2nd and 1st *kyu*)

Students who demonstrate proficiency in all the basic elements of their art become eligible to test for black belt. *Shodan,* literally "first step," is the Japanese word for black belt and signifies that the player has now learned enough about the art to make a start on penetrating its true depths. At the *shodan* level, the practitioner should be able to begin to lead classes and to teach others effectively. In theory, black belt levels proceed all the way to 10th *dan*. However, the term *sensei* ("respected teacher or master") is not normally used until *sandan*, third degree black belt, has been attained. The title *shihan* (Grandmaster/model teacher) is used at the *shichidan* (7th-degree) level.

The scoring scheme in chess is known as the Elo system, after its inventor, Professor Arpad Elo, the Hungarian-born American mathematician. To acquire the title of International Master or Grandmaster, a player must achieve results (known as "norms") in international competitions. The number of points required for a norm in an event is calculated according to the strength of the opposition. In a very strong tournament, for example, it may be necessary to score only 50 percent of the possible points to gain a Grandmaster norm. In a weaker tournament, a player might need as much as 75 percent. Usually three norms are needed to qualify a player for the title.

The relative strengths of the world's leading players are reflected in a twice-yearly ranking list issued by the World Chess Federation (FIDE). On the Elo scale Garry Kasparov stands out as the strongest player in the history of the game.

The benchmark playing levels are as follows:

	Chess ranking	Martial arts equivalent
2800	Garry Kasparov	10th-degree Black Belt
2700	World Champion level	9th-degree Black Belt
2685	Nigel Short	8th-degree Black Belt
2600	Strong grandmaster	8th-degree Black Belt
2500	Grandmaster	*Shihan* level (7th-degree Black Belt)
2400	International Master	4th–6th-degree Black Belt
2300	FIDE Master	*Sensei* level (3rd-degree Black Belt)
2200	U.S. Life Master	2nd-degree Black Belt

2000	Internationally rated	*Shodan* (Black Belt 1st *dan*)
1600	Good club level	Brown Belt
1200	Advanced beginner	Green Belt
<1200	Beginner	White Belt (6th and 5th *kyus*)

Bruce Lee, the greatest modern popularizer of martial arts.

PART II

WHITE BELT CHESS

4

THE BASICS OF CHESS

Chess is a battle of the mind fought between two armies of sixteen pieces. You win when you ensnare, "knock out," or checkmate the opposing king, or when your opponent accepts that his or her position is hopeless and that he must therefore resign.

White to play

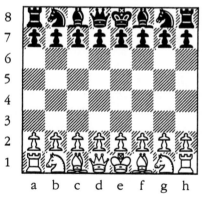

The battlefield or "ring" is a checkered board of sixty-four alternate light and dark squares. At the start of the game, each player's pieces are arranged in rows along the first two ranks, with a light square at the bottom right side of the board. The infantry—the pawns—occupy the front rank; behind them stand the more powerful pieces in the positions shown on page 43.

At the start of the game, White always moves first, then Black; thereafter each side takes alternate moves. The players may move whichever piece they choose according to the conventions described in the following pages.

Capturing

After the initial moves, the two armies advance into combat. It is a basic rule of chess that two pieces cannot occupy the same square simultaneously. When a unit moves to a square already occupied by an enemy piece, a capture takes place and the original occupier is killed, i.e., removed from the board. You may not capture a unit belonging to your own side.

In contrast with checkers, there is no rule insisting that you must accept every opportunity to capture, unless to do so is the only way to save your king from check or checkmate.

Draws

You may not miss a turn. If either player is unable to make a legal move, the result is either checkmate or a draw by "stalemate."

The game can end in a draw at any time by mutual agreement. A draw may also be declared if the position has become sterile and it is obvious that there can be no decisive result, e.g., when there are just lone kings left on the board.

Stalemate occurs when the player whose turn it is to move, not being in checkmate, cannot play a legal move. The result is a draw.

Phases of the Game

There are three main phases: the **opening,** when both players establish their early positions; the **middlegame,** when they try to "develop" their pieces to command the board; and the **endgame,** when a weakened enemy is pursued to the death.

Two rules must be borne in mind at every stage:

- Always look out for snap checkmates, for or against you.
- Always capture your opponent's pieces when it is safe to do so.

Reading the Game:
Simplified Modern Notation

The chess moves described in this book are given according to the universally recognized system of Simplified Modern Notation. This easy-to-learn system of coordinates will be familiar to anyone who has ever used a road map or an A–Z street guide. The vertical lines of squares running from top to bottom of the board as you play are called files. Each of these is identified by a letter. The horizontal lines are called ranks, and each one has a number.

Using these two coordinates, you can instantly identify any square on the board. In the diagram on page 46, the square marked with an "X" is c4.

Board diagrams always appear with Black at the top, White at the bottom.

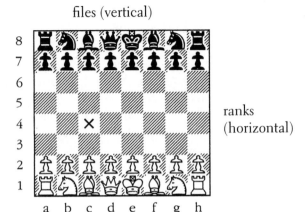

Setting up to play

White moves first, then Black. The white queen always starts on a white square. The black queen always starts on a dark square. A white square must always be at each player's bottom right hand.

Piece moves

The pieces on the first rank are all identified by a figurine: ♔-King, ♕-Queen, ♖-Rook, ♘-Knight, ♗-Bishop. The first item of information given in recording a move is the move number— 1,2,3,4,5, and so on. Next comes the initial letter identifying the piece; then the coordinates of the square from which it moves; then the coordinates of the square on which it lands. Thus, in the diagrams on page 47, White's opening move would be recorded as 1 ♘g1-f3 and Black's response as ♘b8-c6.

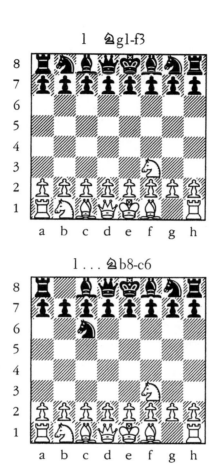

1   ♘g1-f3

1 . . . ♘b8-c6

Pawn moves

A pawn move is not usually prefaced with the initial ♙. The notation 1 d2-d4 indicates that White opened by moving the pawn on square d2 to square d4.

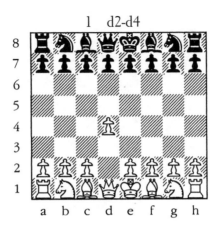

1   d2-d4

Captures

A move resulting in a capture is recorded in the same way, except that the capture is indicated by the addition of a letter x. The diagrams below and at the top of page 49 show the pieces before and after the capture. After the moves

1   e2-e4   e7-e5
2   ♘g1-f3   ♞b8-c6

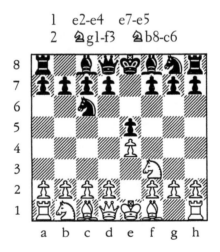

3   d2-d4

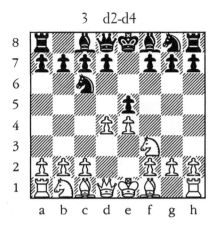

Black now plays the capture.

3 . . . e5xd4

Beginners often fight shy of captures and recaptures for no apparent reason. In the diagram above White's best move is to take the pawn back at once with 4 ♘f3xd4.

It is good to practice capturing, so here are some sequences from openings in which you can try this out. If you are a complete beginner, unsure as yet how the pieces move, take a second look at our advice here after you have thoroughly familiarized yourself with the piece moves (see page 47).

Take back the pawn

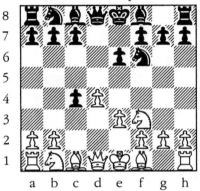

In this position, White is a pawn down. His best move is to take back the pawn at once with ♗f1xc4. If White delays this, there is a very real danger that Black will defend his extra pawn with ... b7-b5.

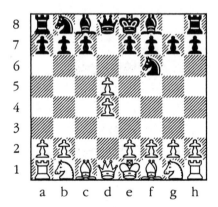

This is a very common position, especially in simultaneous displays. It is Black to move, and he does best to regain his pawn at once with 1 ... ♘f6xd5. Co-author Ray Keene has played numerous games in displays against opponents who either give up another pawn with ... e7-e6 (wrong) or delay the recapture with 1 ... ♗c8-f5 when 2 f2-f3 threatens e2-e4, so cementing White's extra pawn and making it very difficult for Black to reestablish material equality.

You can accelerate your learning process by recording your games using Simplified Modern Notation.

THE VALUE OF THE PIECES

It is essential to understand that weight of numbers decides most chess games. This should never be forgotten. Either through good play, or an opponent's carelessness, at one point in the game one player will often have a distinct material advantage over the other. Although there are exceptions (notably the so-called Immortal Game, see page 184), almost always the player with the larger army wins the day. Even at beginner's level, the loss of a piece without compensation usually results in defeat. In master games the loss of even a single pawn can be disastrous.

But it is not simply the number of surviving pieces that counts, for not all have the same value. A queen is worth more than one rook; rooks are usually more powerful than bishops or knights. So is it possible to quantify the precise strengths of the pieces? This question is of practical as well as academic interest, because often in game situations you will be faced with the possibility of offering part of your own force in order to capture part of your opponent's. You then have to decide whether the exchange would be to your advantage. This table is the basis of many of the most important decisions on the chessboard.

♙	Pawn	= 1
♘	Knight	= 3
♗	Bishop	= 3
♖	Rook	= 5
♕	Queen	= 9
♔	King	is priceless since checkmate ends the game

Although in most situations the pawn is worth only one point, its value can increase dramatically as it advances down the board to become a queen. When a pawn reaches the back rank, it can augment its value from one to nine points in just one move, by promoting. So if you have a passed pawn that is close to queening, guard it with your life. Conversely, if one of your opponent's pawns is thundering toward your own back rank, do everything you can to block or capture it.

SHARPENING YOUR SWORD: HOW THE PIECES MOVE AND CAPTURE

The pieces, and the rules, of chess have been constant since the fifteenth century.

The pawns

Each player has eight pawns, which begin in a line across the board on the second and seventh ranks, respectively. They are the foot soldiers of the chess army and move in only one direction: forward. Pawns normally move one square at a time along the file; see the black pawn in the diagram below, where squares marked with an "x" show the moves open to the pawns.

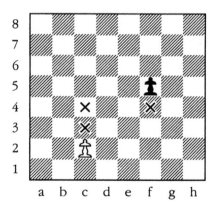

An exception is made for each pawn's first move — and only the first move. Here it has the option of advancing two squares along the file instead of one. (See White's pawn on c2 in the diagram on page 52.)

When they capture, pawns have a quite different action, moving one square forward diagonally. In the diagram below, White can take either Black's pawn or his knight, and the black pawn can take the white pawn. As we shall see, when a pawn reaches the opponent's back rank, it promotes to a queen.

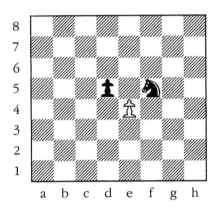

The rook

Each player has two rooks, positioned in the corner squares. The English word "rook" is idiosyncratic. Most other European languages use the word for "castle" or "tower" (French *tour*, German *Turm*, Italian and Spanish *torre*). The probable derivation is from *rocco*, an alternative Italian word for tower, or from *rukh*, the ancient Persian word for a war chariot. In Russia the piece is known as *ladya*, "boat." Children in England and the United States often use the more descriptive "castle." The squares to which the rook can legally move are marked with an "x."

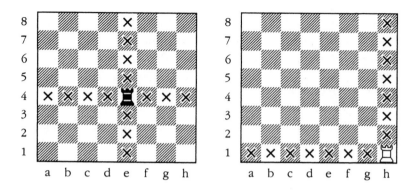

Rooks move only along ranks and files, never along diagonals. A rook can travel as many squares as it likes in either direction along a rank or file in a single move, provided nothing blocks its path. It captures in the usual way, by moving on to its victim's square.

The rook is an important weapon, second in value only to the queen, with one significant strategic advantage over the other pieces. Though it often makes better tactical sense to mobilize rooks toward the center of the board, they are also effective at or near the edge, where they can still command the same number of squares.

The bishop

Each player has two bishops, one placed on a white square and one on a black. Of all the pieces on the board, the bishop has the most colorful history. In *chaturanga* it was depicted as an elephant, one of the four branches of the Indian army. In Russian the bishop is still called *slon*, elephant. Almost as soon as the game spread into Europe (where elephants were not so familiar) in the tenth century, the piece took on a variety of guises. In Germany it became a *Laufer* (runner or messenger); in France a *fou* (fool or court jester).

The bishops sweep along the chessboard on the diagonals (see diagrams on page 55). As long as no other piece restricts their path, they can move to any square along the chosen diagonal route. They cannot leap over pieces in their path, but they can capture by landing on a square occupied by an enemy piece; thus White's bishop can take Black's pawn (left below). Black's bishop, on the other hand, cannot attack the white pawn (right below). It is vitally important to remember that a bishop must start and end its move on squares of the same color. If you move a bishop from a light square to a dark square, something has gone seriously wrong and you must try the move again.

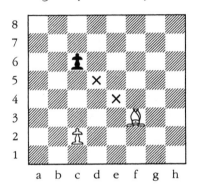 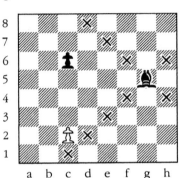

The knight

Each player has two knights, positioned on the squares next to the rooks. They are the ancient warhorses of *chaturanga* transformed into medieval knights, the universally recognized symbols of feudal chivalry. For knights of chivalry, however, they are remarkably devious. The knight is the only piece on the board that is always allowed to jump over occupied squares. Its movement is composed of two separate steps. First it makes one step of a single square in any direction along a rank or file. Then, still moving away from the square of departure, it makes a second step of a single square on a diagonal. It can do this even if it is totally surrounded by other pieces — whether friendly or hostile — and captures in exactly the same way as it moves.

Because of its unusual movement, a sudden knight attack often causes havoc in the enemy camp. The knights' range is severely limited at the edge of the board, and they are much more effective deployed toward the center. *Springer*, their German name, is the most suggestive of their character. In French they are called *cavaliers*; in Italian *cavallos*; and in Spanish *caballos*. In contrast with the bishop, when you make a move with the knight, it always finishes on a different-color square from its starting square. If a knight is on white, it must move to black, and vice versa.

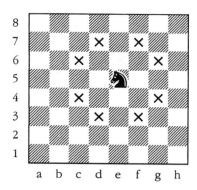 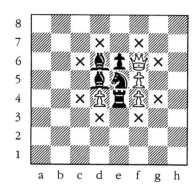

Knight exercises

The knight move is the most difficult to grasp and is therefore worth practicing. In the diagram at the top of page 57 try to work out the fastest route for the white knight to reach e5 (x) and for the black knight to reach f5 (+).

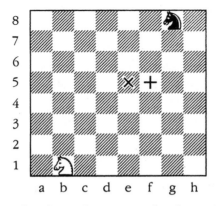

Answer: White's knight on b1 can reach e5 via a3 and c4 or d2 and f3 (or c4). The black knight can travel most speedily to f5 via e7 or h6. Now try out other knight moves for yourself.

The queen

Each player has one queen at the start of the game. As we have seen, her ancestor in early Indian and Arabic forms was a "minister" or "vizier" with only a hobbling range of movement; one adjacent diagonal square was the limit. Not until 1475 was the queen given her vast firepower—the chess equivalent of long-range field artillery—and as a result launched the game played today.

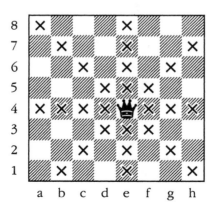

The role of the queen, the strongest and most mobile piece on the board, is so important that it is scarcely exaggerating to say that if you win your opponent's queen, you have won the game. She may move along any rank, file, or diagonal in any direction for as many squares as she chooses. She may not turn corners, nor move through, or on to, a square occupied by a friendly unit. Neither can she move through a square held by an enemy, though she can move on to such a square and capture the occupier. As the diagram at the bottom of page 57 shows, a centrally placed queen has a theoretical range of no fewer than 27 possible moves in eight directions; this is a crucial factor in attacking enemy pieces and in planning and executing checkmates. The queen is a very powerful attacking piece.

The king

Each player has one king, which is the most important, though not the most powerful, piece on the board. The prime objective of chess is to surround and pin down the enemy king—i.e., to deliver checkmate. Yet the king's move itself is very simple: one square in any direction.

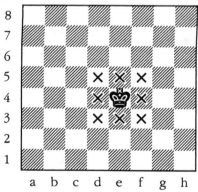

The one exception, called castling, is not essential to a beginner's game, and we shall postpone discussing it. In the game's early stages, the king is not generally used in attack. To attack an enemy unit he must move on to a neighboring square—far too risky when he can retreat to safety only one square at a time. It is only in the later stages, the endgame, when most of the pieces have been removed through captures and the risk of a snap checkmate has diminished, that the king emerges as a fighter. Earlier on his role tends to be purely defensive. The king's maneuverability is seriously reduced if he is placed at the edge of the board—which can be ruthlessly exploited in the endgame. Often the first stage in delivering checkmate is to force the enemy king against the edge, cutting off all his lines of escape.

CHECK AND CHECKMATE

The object of the game is to ensnare your opponent's king—to "give checkmate." Checkmate may be achieved in innumerable different ways, using your attacking pieces in a wide variety of combinations. Some checkmates—almost all in games played by Grandmasters—are the result of long-range strategic planning, patience, and guile. The giving of check underlines the special nature of the king in chess. A king is said to be in check when it is threatened by an opposing unit—i.e., when that unit's next move would result in its capture.

A player whose king is in check must remove it from danger. If this is not possible, checkmate has occurred and the game is over. It is illegal either to put or to keep your own king in check.

Escaping from check

There are three ways of evading check.

1. By moving the king out of harm's way. But remember that you may not move it to another square on which it would also be in check.
2. By capturing the enemy piece that delivers the check.
3. By interposing a friendly unit to block the check (except in the case of a knight check).

If you can stop a check in more than one way, choose the move you think best.

Announcing check

If a player is in check and plays a move that fails to stop it, he has moved illegally and must retract. To save their opponents from this kind of embarrassment, most players (except in formal tournaments) courteously announce that they have played a checking move by saying "check" as they put down the piece.

It is also customary to indicate a check when writing down a move. This is done by adding the symbol + to the normal description of the move, as in ♗a5-d8+ (below), where White's king is in check from Black's bishop and must therefore move. The crosses indicate the squares that are legal refuges.

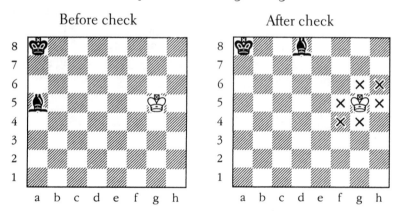

Before check   After check

In the diagram at the top of page 61, White's king is in check from Black's queen on b4. There are three ways of stopping the check:

1. White can move his king with ♔e1f1 or ♔e1e2 or ♔e1d1.
2. White can take the Black queen with ♕b7xb4.
3. White can interpose a piece to block the check. There are six moves to achieve this, namely, c2c3, ♘b1c3, ♘b1d2, ♗c1d2, ♖h3-c3, and ♖a3-c3.

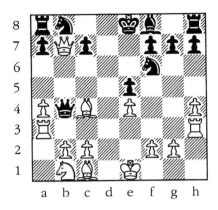

Of these choices, White's only good move is the second, ♛b7xb4. Otherwise, Black's queen will capture White's, achieving an overwhelming material advantage of nine points.

The diagram below shows check. White can escape by moving his king to g2 or h2.

The next case is terminal. As in the previous diagram, White is in check from the black rook, but here there is no escape route. It is checkmate. White's pawns trap his own king.

Checkmate by the knight

A dramatic "smothered mate" with the knight imprisoning Black's king, which has become trapped by its own defensive cordon. Although Black has a huge material advantage of rook and queen against knight, White's knight has delivered the death blow.

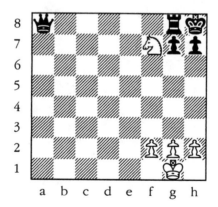

Checkmate by knight and bishop

The white pieces conspire to deprive Black's king of any escape squares. There is no question of the black king being trapped by its own forces—the white army simply takes away all the flight squares.

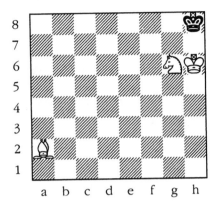

Checkmate by the queen

A typical checkmating motif with the white queen in the main role. Here the black king is trapped by its own pieces. Playing a queen to h7 (or, if you were Black, h2) is a common way of delivering checkmate against a castled king. Watch out for these queen swoops. Try to create opportunities for them, but make sure you do not get caught by one yourself.

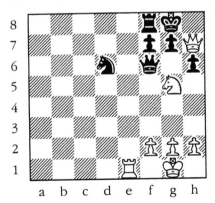

Mate by the rook

Although material is equal, Black has fallen for a real sucker punch. This example of checkmate by a rook on the back rank (which we have already encountered in a simpler form) is one of the most common types. Always keep an eye out for it if your king, or your opponent's, does not have a bolthole in the pawns around it. If you have moved your king to the kingside, behind an apparently unassailable wall of pawns, a very sensible precaution is to move one pawn forward at some stage, just to make some air for your king.

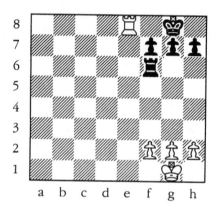

THREE SPECIAL CASES

Now that you are familiar with the game's basic rules, it is time to look at some special rules that are often used but apply only in specific situations. They are easily understood and vital to the development of your game.

Castling

This maneuver governs the behavior of your king when acting in concert with your rooks. Castling consists of moving your king two squares along the back rank toward either your king's rook or your queen's rook, depending on which side you wish to castle. You then move the relevant rook to the square through which the king has just passed. (The diagrams on page 66 illustrate the various options.) Castling is extremely important, representing the symbolic entry of the king into his fortress.

It is wise to castle early in all your games. There are two important advantages. Castling is a vital means of moving a rook quickly to the center, where it can be most useful; and it takes the king immediately away from the center, where it is vulnerable.

Depending on whether the king's rook or the queen's rook is used, we speak of castling kingside or queenside (see diagrams). Castling is the only move in which two of your own pieces can move simultaneously. You may castle only if the king and the rook involved have not made previous moves and remain on their starting positions; and also only if the squares between the king and the rook have been vacated and are unoccupied.

There are two additional conditions:

1. The king may not castle if it is in check, nor may it castle into check.
2. Castling is prohibited if the square through which the king passes (i.e., the square on which the rook finishes) is under attack from an enemy unit.

Note that it is possible to castle if the rook is threatened. Queenside castling is also permitted even if square b1 (or, in Black's case, b8) is under fire.

In chess notation, kingside castling for both White and Black is written as 0-0. Queenside castling is given as 0-0-0. The finer points of chess etiquette dictate that in castling you move the king first.

Before White castles kingside

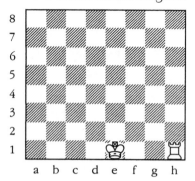

After White castles kingside

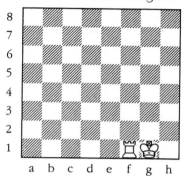

Before Black castles queenside

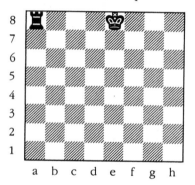

After Black castles queenside

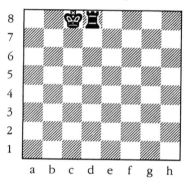

Pawn promotion

The art of shepherding a passed pawn through to promotion is a vital key to victory. As the game progresses, the pawns move down the board away from their starting squares. If a pawn successfully runs the gauntlet all the way to the eighth rank, for White, or to the first rank, for Black, it has gone as far as it can go and runs out of normal moves. A dramatic transformation then occurs. The player who owns the pawn must upgrade it to a higher rank of his own choosing—knight, bishop, rook, or queen, though not king. This process is called promotion or, more commonly, queening the pawn, since in actual play one almost always chooses to promote to a queen.

Subsequently the newly promoted pawn behaves exactly as if it were a "natural" queen, or whatever other piece was chosen. Thus theoretically (though one cannot imagine it happening in practice) one player could have as many as nine queens on the board at the same time. In chess parlance, a pawn is called a "passed pawn" when no hostile pawn can impede its progress to becoming a queen. For a pawn to be truly "passed," there must be no enemy pawn in front of it, either on its own file or in the files on each side of it, as shown in the two diagrams below.

 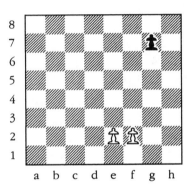

The a7, c2, and e2 pawns are passed. Those on f2 and g7 are not.

One reason for not queening the pawn is if promotion to knight would immediately give checkmate, as shown on page 68.

1 f7-f8 = ♘ is instant checkmate. Promoting to a queen would lead only to a draw by stalemate.

The en passant rule

This rule prescribes a situation in which a pawn may capture another in a different way from normal. The possibility of an *en passant* capture (shown as "ep" in chess notation) arises only when a pawn on its starting square takes advantage of its optional initial move of two squares forward. If an enemy pawn is so placed that it could have captured the pawn if it had moved only one square forward, it does not lose the opportunity to do so. In this instance, therefore, it captures by passing one square diagonally behind the target pawn, rather than on to the square it is occupying. The diagrams show how this move works.

It is important to remember that the right to capture en passant lasts for only one move. You must take immediately, or not at all.

The two diagrams on page 69 illustrate the *en passant* rule; "x" marks the spot of capture. If Black is to move and he plays . . . g7-g5, White's right to capture remains exactly the same as it would have been if Black had played . . . g7-g6. White can still take on g6. Similarly, if White plays d2-d4, Black may capture by playing . . . c4xd3 ep.

En passant in action

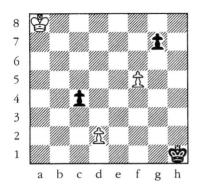 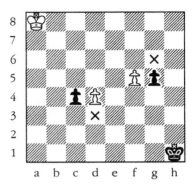

There is no obligation to capture *en passant*; it is entirely the player's choice whether to do so or not. Furthermore, there is no need to agree before the game that *en passant* captures are an option. *En passant* is an integral part of the rules of chess; if you make an *en passant* capture, and your opponent complains that it was not agreed to before the game started, simply ignore him. *En passant* may turn out to be a gamewinner, so always remember it.

CHOOSING WHITE AND BLACK

If you are new to chess, you may not know the correct procedure for deciding who plays White or Black. Since White starts first, the white player enjoys a certain initiative, but this is only pronounced at the highest levels, where it is much like the advantage of the tennis serve.

In a tournament or match, colors are always preordained by drawing lots. In more social circumstances, the stronger player normally takes Black in the first game, with the colors alternating thereafter. If you and your opponent's relative strengths are unknown, one player (it does not matter which) should volunteer to take one white pawn and one black pawn, shuffle them without the opponent seeing, and then hold them out, concealing each pawn in a grip. The opponent makes a blind choice and for the first game takes the color of the pawn picked from the closed hand.

An Arabic legend says that the inventor of chess was invited by a grateful emperor to name his own reward. The man modestly asked for a quantity of corn—one grain for the first square of the chessboard, two for the second, four for the third, and so on, doubling each time—and the emperor readily agreed.

When the court mathematicians got to work on the problem, the demand proved not to be as modest as it had seemed. The number of grains on the board was about 18,000,000,000,000,000,000, payment for which would have been enough to bankrupt a number of empires.

Nobody supposes that the legend is true, but it does offer an inkling of chess's limitless variety. A Grandmaster game is classed as a "miniature" if it lasts only 25 or fewer moves per player. If every possible game, even of this restricted kind, were reproduced in books of same page size and type size as the London or New York telephone directories, the result would cover the entire surface of the earth and then spread out, filling all available space to a distance in every direction equal to that from earth to the farthest known galaxy—not once, but 100,000,000,000,000,000,000 times.

5

DRAWING THE SWORD—
THE CLASSIC OPENINGS

Chess is a game of virtually infinite possibilities. Not all the computing power in the world could calculate all the possible moves in all the possible games that could ever be played. Yet for all this richness and variety, there are a number of well-trodden pathways and strategic schemes around which most players build their games. Even novice players quickly come to understand that some squares on the board are more important than others, and that success depends on seizing control of them quickly.

This chapter looks at the crucial question of the opening, the initial phase of the game, in which the players joust for territorial and tactical control. Some of the commonest openings, favored by Grandmasters and amateurs alike, are set out for you to learn, practice, and improvise upon. The next two chapters introduce you to the middlegame—the most open aspect of chess—and, to make sure that you can finish what you have started, to some of the classic methods of using just a few pieces to push a strategic advantage and arrive at a decisive conclusion in the endgame.

THE FASTEST KILL

The most rapid possible game of chess resulting in checkmate is called Fool's Mate—a trick possible to perform only on a complete beginner. Nobody would ever make the same mistake twice. The game is over in just two moves, shown in the diagrams below.

White plays 1 g2-g4
Black responds 1 . . . e7-e6

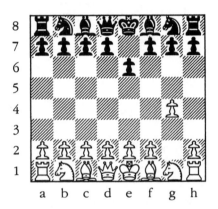

White continues with 2 f2-f4
and Black checkmates with 2 . . . ♛d8-h4

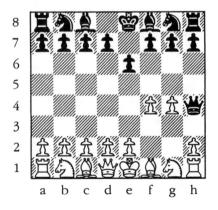

A much more common trap for beginners is Scholar's Mate. It is well worth committing the sequence of moves to memory.

1	e2-e4	e7-e5
2	♗f1-c4	♝f8-c5
3	♕d1-h5	♞b8-c6

The threat to e5 has been spotted, but not to f7. And now a horrible shock:

4	♕h5xf7 mate

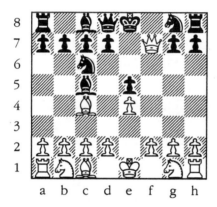

White delivers the *coup de grâce*. Black's king has no escape route, and none of his other pieces is in a position to attack the white queen. Black has failed in the very basics of chess and martial arts strategy. He has failed to spot White's threats, and has also failed to ensure the safety of his king.

This is not something, in its pure and undisguised form, to try against an experienced player. Mate will easily be averted, and you will find your opponent's emerging pieces harrying your queen all over the board. However, the principle of the weak or blind spot on f7 is important. It often proves to be the focus of a successful attack.

Keep the forces concentrated in an overpowering mass.

—Karl von Clausewitz, *On War*, 1873

Aiming at the enemy

In kendo, the sword is drawn quickly and aimed directly at the enemy's center line. Any delay in unsheathing it puts the combatant at a distinct disadvantage. The same is true of chess. Pieces must be mobilized quickly and "aimed" at the enemy's king via the center of the board.

The key precepts are:

1. Move one or two center pawns early on.
2. Castle your king as quickly as possible.
3. Develop knights and bishops quickly.

The following three typical sequences show both sides observing these rules. Note how important central play is in all these examples.

Ruy Lopez Opening

1	e2-e4	e7-e5
2	♘g1-f3	♘b8-c6
3	♗f1-b5	d7-d6
4	0-0	

Queen's Gambit Declined

1	d2-d4	d7-d5
2	c2-c4	e7-e6
3	♘b1-c3	♘g8-f6
4	♘g1-f3	♗f8-e7

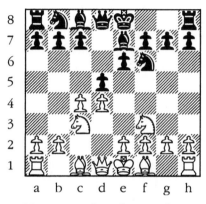

Nimzowitsch-Indian Defense

1	d2-d4	♘g8-f6
2	c2-c4	e7-e6
3	♘b1-c3	♗f8-b4

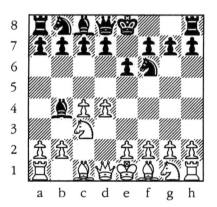

GOOD PAWN STRUCTURE

During the opening you should aim to occupy the center with your pawns. The strategic purpose of controlling as many of the center squares as possible is to restrict your opponent's freedom.

Remember that, for their first move only, pawns can move forward two squares instead of one. Well-placed pawns can also be most effective in harrying exposed enemy pieces.

Study the moves in the following example:

1	e2-e4	c7-c6
2	d2-d4	d7-d5
3	e4-e5	

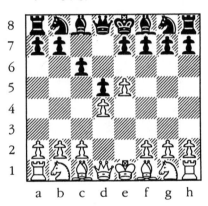

Here White has already succeeded in cramping Black by taking away the development square f6 from his king's knight. Nonetheless, this is a recognized opening, the Caro-Kann Defense.

In the following example, Black's play is highly unorthodox.

1	e2-e4	♞ g8-f6
2	e4-e5	♞ f6-e4
3	d2-d3	♞ e4-c5
4	d3-d4	♞ c5-e6
5	d4-d5	

Black's opening has been a total disaster. White has been allowed to gain time by kicking the black knight around, with the result that White now has excellent central control with two of his pawns.

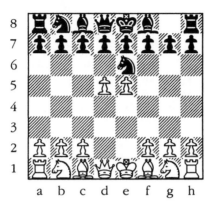

OTHER OPENINGS TO AVOID

These openings do little or nothing to develop your pieces or control the center.

1   h2-h4

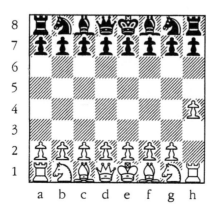

White intends ♗h3, but if Black responds . . . d5 he has the center and his queen's bishop also attacks the h3-square, stopping White's plan.

1   g2-g4

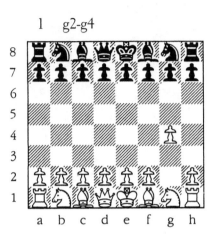

This is too weakening and off center.

1   ♘h3

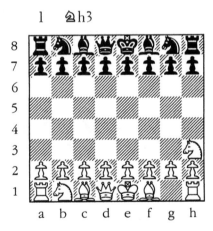

White has developed a piece but, being on the side of the board, the knight does little to help in the fight for the center.

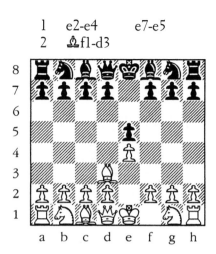

1 e2-e4   e7-e5
2 ♗f1-d3

Here the white bishop on d3 blocks White's own mobilization, rather like getting your sword stuck in your own scabbard!

6

MANEUVERING
FOR MASTERY—
THE MIDDLEGAME

You must make fullest use of your weaponry. It is false not to do so, and to die with a weapon yet undrawn.

—Musashi, *A Book of Five Rings*

Once you have drawn your sword and developed and mobilized all your forces, the opening is over and you enter the middlegame. With your pieces in play all sorts of ploys, stratagems, material winning devices, and sacrificial attacks become possible.

COMBINATIONS AND TRAPS

In boxing, the best-known tactic is "'the old one-two'"—a jab followed instantaneously by a right cross. The best fighters "throw-punches in bunches." These bunches are called combinations and they raise the effectiveness of every strike dramatically. Similarly, the chess player can get the best out of the pieces only by coordinating their movements and using them in combination. Working cooperatively, two or more attacking pieces can be absolutely deadly. It is also vital to look out for combination attacks that your opponent is preparing for you!

Rook combinations

The rook is a long-range piece and operates most effectively when it can directly bombard or penetrate the hostile fortress. Rooks can be especially deadly if they enter the first two ranks of the opponent's position. For a white rook this would be ranks 7 and 8; for a black rook, ranks 1 and 2. Here are some examples:

First, White wins by immediate and violent penetration.

| 1 | ♖h1xh7+ | ♚h8xh7 |
| 2 | ♖f3-h3 | checkmate |

The next example is more complex, revealing the power of a rook entering the back rank.

White: Havasi; Black: Monticelli
Budapest 1929 (variation)

Black's rook is well placed on d1 but has no immediate threat. Meanwhile, Black's queen is attacked. However, Black unleashes the latent power of his rook with the advance 1 . . . b6-b5!! (The chess notation ! signifies a remarkable move, !! one of truly outstanding quality. Likewise ? indicates a very poor move, and ?? a horrific blunder.) This wins White's queen, since Black can ignore the attack on his own queen. 1 . . . b6-b5!! severs the connection between White's queen and knight, thus introducing the possibility of . . . ♖xf1 mate.

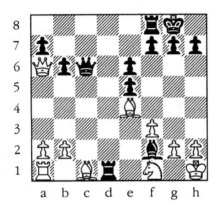

Rooks on the seventh rank

The natural position for a rook to extract its maximum strategic advantage is on the "seventh" rank (any square from a7-h7 for a white rook, conversely the second rank—any square from a2-h2—for a black rook). Examine the position on page 83.

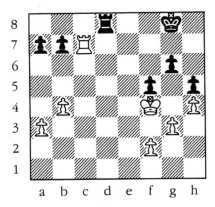

Although material is equal, the fact that White has already established his rook on the seventh rank gives him a huge advantage. Black's pawns start out on the seventh rank, so those still in place on a7 and b7 represent an obvious and ready target for the white rook. Second, the white rook's sweeping action hems in the black king on the back rank and prevents it from advancing to defend its own weak pawns on the king's flank from attack by the white king.

The two chief advantages of a rook established on the seventh rank are attacking enemy pawns and cutting off the enemy king.

Doubled rooks on the seventh

If one rook on the seventh rank is a real pain for your opponent, two rooks that have invaded the seventh rank can act like a murderous, bludgeoning battering-ram, smashing the opponent into submission. Here is a celebrated example, a variation from the game between Nimzowitsch, White, and World Champion Capablanca, Black, played at New York in 1927. Here, the black rooks have rampaged on to White's second rank.

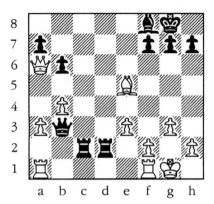

How does Black exploit his doubled rooks on the seventh rank? They represent such a mighty force that Black can even sacrifice his queen:

$$1 \quad \dots \quad \text{♛b3xe3}$$

There is now a double attack against e5 and f2, but if White snatches at the queen with

$$2 \quad \text{f2xe3}$$

then the assassins pour in with

2	...	♜d2-g2+
3	♔g1-h1	♜g2xh2+
4	♔h1-g1	♜c2-g2 checkmate

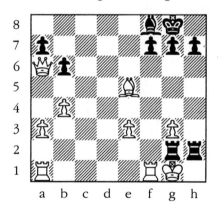

Musashi said, "The strategist makes small things into big things." In chess, once you have created a strategic advantage, such as rooks on the seventh, look for opportunities to translate this into a forcing sequence leading to a decisive material advantage, or to checkmate itself.

The bishop pair

A pair of bishops swooping down adjacent diagonals can be devastatingly dangerous, since they control an extra swath of both light and dark squares. Consider these positions:

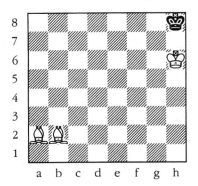

This is checkmate.

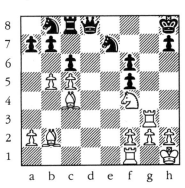

1 ♗b2xf6 is checkmate.

Two bishops can be extraordinarily efficacious in smashing the fortifications around the opponent's king. Here is a classic case, the double bishop sacrifice.

White: Lasker; Black: Bauer
Amsterdam 1889

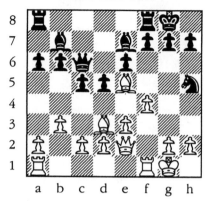

White strikes like lightning from a clear blue sky.

1	♗d3xh7+	♚g8xh7
2	♛e2xh5+	♚h7-g8
3	♗b2xg7	♚g8xg7
4	♛h5-g4+	♚g7-h7
5	♖f1-f3	

Threatening ♖f3-h3 followed by mate. Black's hand is forced.

5	. . .	e6-e5
6	♖f3-h3+	♛c6-h6
7	♖h3xh6+	♚h7xh6
8	♛g4-d7	

forks Black's bishops and wins easily on material.

Legall's mate

Monsieur de Kermur, Sire de Legall, was a French champion in the mid eighteenth century. He specialized in combination play, and originated the mate that bears his name.

1	e2-e4	e7-e5
2	♘g1-f3	d7-d6
3	♗f1-c4	g7-g6
4	♘b1-c3	♗c8-g4

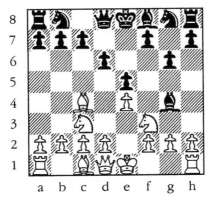

This position looks safe enough for Black (indeed, the juicy prize of the white queen is in the line of fire of Black's bishop), but White has a fiendish combination up his sleeve, with bishop and two knights ready to deliver a startling *coup de grâce*.

5	♘f3xe5	♗g4xd1
6	♗c4xf7+	♔e8-e7
7	♘c3-d5	checkmate

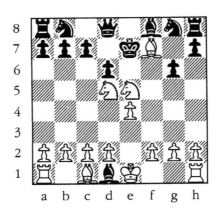

The fork

Karate students train to master the devastating technique of *men-munetsuki*—punching to the head and body simultaneously. When this is delivered properly, the opponent may block one strike, but the other will get through and the match will soon be over. The chess equivalent is the fork: a move that leaves an attacking piece ranged against two or more enemy-held pieces simultaneously. The defender can save one of his two threatened pieces, but not both.

The example below is from Game 10 in the World Championship match played between Tigran Petrosian (White) and Boris Spassky in Moscow in 1966.

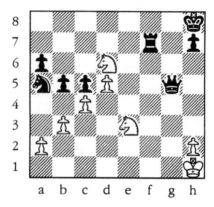

Thirty moves have so far been played, but now White plays:

31 ♘d6xf7+

At this point, Black resigned because White has set up a fork with the knight on d6. Look at what would have happened if Black had tried to play on. His next move is forced upon him to escape check:

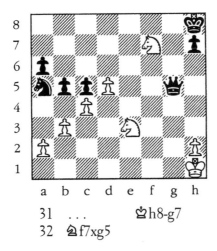

31 …	♚h8-g7
32 ♘f7xg5	

The fork materializes after White's move 31, with the knight on f7 threatening two enemy pieces simultaneously. Black has to move his king to escape check, leaving White to mop up the queen with his next move. White now has a material advantage (an extra knight) that is quite sufficient to ensure victory.

A fork does not only occur when there are just a few pieces left. It may occur at any stage of a game, even at the beginning, as in this example (which occurs after 1 e2-e4 c7-c5 2 ♘g1-f3 d7-d6 3 c2-c3 a7-a6 4 ♗f1-e2 g7-g6 5 0-0 ♗f8-g7 6 h2-h3 ♘g8-f6 7 ♘b1-a3):

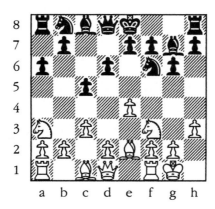

White has left his e-pawn *en prise*—i.e., where it can be captured (by the knight on f6). But if Black swallows the bait with:

7 ... ♘f6xe4

He will find himself caught in a fork, and lose his knight, after:

8 ♕d1-a4+

The fork in action

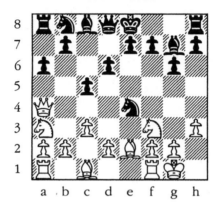

Black must parry the threat to his king when the white queen will capture the black knight on e4, achieving a decisive material advantage of 3 points to 1.

Discovered attack

A discovered attack (often giving check) is one directed by a stationary piece that is "discovered" by the removal of another piece in front of it, as in this example:

1	e2-e4	e7-e6
2	d2-d4	d7-d5
3	e4-e5	c7-c5

4	c2-c3	♞b8-c6
5	♞g1-f3	♛d8-b6
6	♝f1-d3	c5xd4
7	c3xd4	♞g8-e7
8	0-0	♞e7-g6
9	♞b1-c3	

Here White has set a trap that has snared thousands of victims.

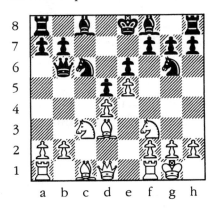

The bait for Black is the white d-pawn, which is open to attack from the knight on c6. It is bait that Black will accept at his peril . . .

9	. . .	♞c6xd4
10	♞f3xd4	♛b6xd4
11	♝d3-b5+	

The bishop biding its time on d3 poses no obvious threat until the exchange of pieces on the d4 square in front of it. This lures the black queen out of position into the center of the board and opens the way for the white queen on d1 to launch a deadly attack on the black queen. White will soon play ♛d1xd4 and win easily on the basis of his huge material advantage.

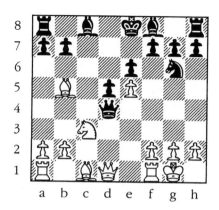

The pin

The pin is one of the most useful and devastating tactical devices. It is especially valuable to pin and thus immobilize a piece against an opponent's king. Consider the following position.

Black to move

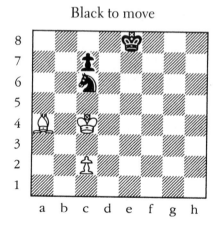

The white bishop on a4 pins the black knight to the black king. The knight cannot move because the black king would be in check. Black, to move, has only one defense. He must play 1 . . .

♚e8-d7 to defend the knight, but he is still in the pin. Given one more move, namely . . . ♞d7-d6, Black would break the pin, his knight would regain its freedom to move, and the game would be a draw.

Unfortunately for Black, White to play could decisively augment the pressure against the black knight with 2 ♗c4-c5 or 2 ♗c4-d5. The two-one attack against Black's pinned knight on c6 now wins material and the game for White.

The skewer

The skewer is another deadly and common tactical device, generally involving an X-ray attack through a more valuable piece, winning a lesser unit in terrain to the rear. Consider the following position with White to move:

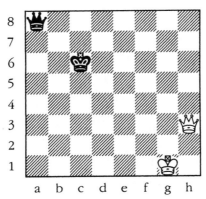

In such a simplified situation, with no apparent danger lurking, a draw would seem inevitable. However, given that it is White's move, he can exploit his initiative to establish his queen on the long light-squared diagonal, giving check to the black king. Thus, 1 ♕h3-g2+, the black king must now step out of the X-ray attack, e.g., 1 . . . ♚c6-c7 when White picks up Black's skewered queen with 2 ♕g2xa8, gaining an easy win on material.

7

THE CLEANEST KILLS— BASIC ENDGAMES

It is not very nice, but the plain truth is that the most successful fighters possess a "killer instinct." Known as "finishers," they relentlessly seek their foe's demise. All World Chess Champions share this instinct. In chess, there is no point in knowing how to begin a game unless you also learn how to end one. For all practical purposes the variations in endgames are infinite, yet a number of common situations arise again and again. Some of the more complex ways of delivering checkmate will be explained later. Here we consider some of the basic methods of "finishing" your opponent after you have achieved a material advantage.

KING AND QUEEN VERSUS KING

It is essential to know the basic mating positions of king and queen against lone king. The first and most important rule in this very common type of endgame is that you must drive the enemy king to one of the four sides of the board. This is the chess equivalent of having your opponent "on the ropes." If you fail to do this, you will not be able to give checkmate.

These two diagrams show standard checkmating positions:

Black king is checkmated   Black king is checkmated

 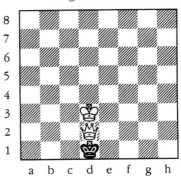

The drive to the edge

It is useful practice to try out some endgames against an opponent, either human or a computer program. Here is a typical mating process in an endgame of king and queen versus king:

White must push back the black king

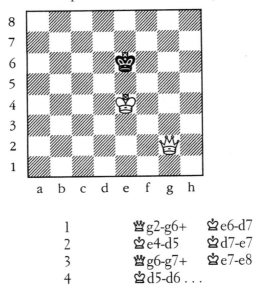

1	♕g2-g6+	♚e6-d7
2	♔e4-d5	♚d7-e7
3	♕g6-g7+	♚e7-e8
4	♔d5-d6 . . .	

Checkmate is imminent.

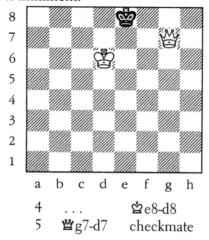

4	...	♚e8-d8
5	♕g7-d7	checkmate

KING AND ROOK VERSUS KING

This is just as common as king and queen versus king, and the mating positions should also be memorized. As you can see from the next two diagrams, it is again essential to drive the king to one of the four sides of the board; otherwise it will escape.

White king checkmated   Black king checkmated

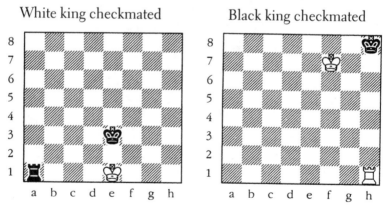

The drive to the edge

It is good practice to set up a board with just the king and rook in play. Then work through some checkmating sequences. So often promising players conduct an excellent game, emerge with the potentially crushing advantage of king and rook versus king, and then fail to press home the win through ignorance of the necessity to drive the enemy king to one of the four edges.

White must push back the black king

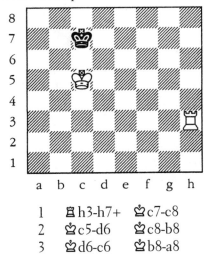

1	♖h3-h7+	♚c7-c8
2	♔c5-d6	♚c8-b8
3	♔d6-c6	♚b8-a8

Checkmate imminent

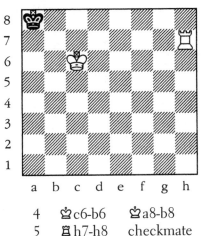

4	♔c6-b6	♚a8-b8
5	♖h7-h8	checkmate

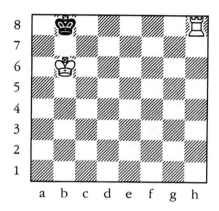

KING AND PAWN VERSUS KING

This is one of the most frequent and important endgames. It is of great benefit to know which positions are drawn and which can be won. In some cases, the lone king will be so far away from the pawn that the pawn can romp home and become a queen—an easy win. But what if the lone king can block the pawn's path? You might think that your king should shepherd the pawn home to become a queen in all cases. Sometimes this is so, but not always. The odds on a win and a draw in king and pawn versus king are about 50:50.

Should White advance the pawn?

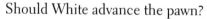
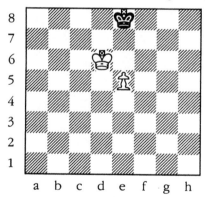

Let us look at a typical example. The reward for learning the principle will be to pick up a lot of extra points in marginal endgames. Attention to detail is essential in both chess and the martial arts—and indeed in business and any walk of life where you aim to succeed, excel, and win!

In the previous diagram, it is White's move. White can win, but the question is how. The obvious way is to advance the pawn and try to make a queen. However, this is too crude and does not work. Let us see why.

1	e5-e6	♚e8-d8
2	e6-e7+	♚d8-e8
3	♔d6-e6	

As we can see from the next diagram, the result is a draw by stalemate (see pages 102–106). The black king is not in checkmate but cannot make a legal move.

Draw by stalemate

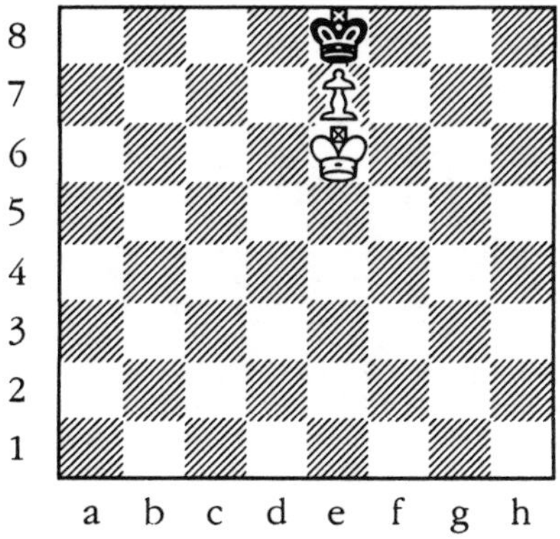

The way to win is to place your king directly in front of your opponent's king, forcing it to give way. "Gaining the opposition," as this maneuver is called, is the most vital principle for endgames of kings and pawns, and you will win only if you remember it. This is how White should have played the ending:

1	♔d6-e6	♚e8-f8
2	♔e6-d7	♚f8-f7

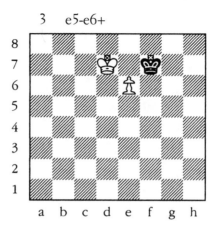

3   e5-e6+

It becomes obvious that Black cannot prevent the pawn from queening. There is one equally simple alternative version.

1	♔d6-e6	♚e8-d8
2	♔e6-f7	♚d8-d7
3	e5-e6+	

Now the pawn will promote.

Once again, the pawn will inevitably queen. In all king and pawn versus king endings, the weaker side could draw if it were possible to pass without making a move. Unfortunately for Black, this is illegal.

8

DEFINING DEADLOCK— IF YOU CAN'T WIN . . .

Chess is not a game of chance. Games are usually played to a "genuine" result, and the better player usually wins. However, with players of a similar ability, the genuine result may be that neither can gain a decisive advantage and the game must end in a draw.

Types of Draw

Draws can come about in a number of ways, some of them quite complex, which it is important to know.

Agreement

This is the commonest kind of draw. Both players agree that the game is unwinnable, and draw by consent.

Threefold repetition

If exactly the same position occurs three times in a game, with the same player to move each time, the game is drawn.

Perpetual check

A situation in which one player continues to give various checks that his opponent, although not checkmated, cannot escape. The game is then drawn either by agreement or by threefold repetition.

Fifty-move rule

If no pieces are captured, and no pawns moved, for a sequence of 50 moves by each player, the result is a draw. This rule is not often invoked.

Insufficient mating material

Some endgame positions are drawn simply because there are insufficient pieces left on the board to give checkmate. Here are some examples:

1. King against king is a draw. As they cannot occupy squares adjacent to each other, they cannot even give check.
2. King and bishop against a lone king is always a draw; no mating positions are possible.
3. King and knight against a lone king is always a draw; no mating positions are possible.
4. King and two knights against a lone king is also (amazingly) a draw, but only if the weaker side defends correctly. Checkmates are possible.
5. King and pawn against lone king, a common endgame, is sometimes a draw. As we have seen, it depends on the relative positions of the kings.

STALEMATE

This common form of draw occurs if one player, not being in checkmate, runs out of legal moves. It is most likely to happen in an endgame when one player has only a king left on the board, and can occur even when one side has a material advantage.

Common stalemating positions

White to move: stalemate

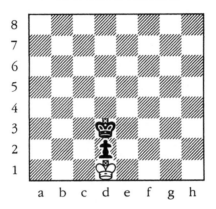

White is not in checkmate but has no legal moves. On c1 or e1 he would be in check to the pawn. On c2 or e2 he would be on an adjacent square (and in check) to the king. This is stalemate.

White to move: stalemate

Here any move by White would put him in check to the queen. Despite Black's clear material advantage, the result is a draw by stalemate.

Black to move: stalemate

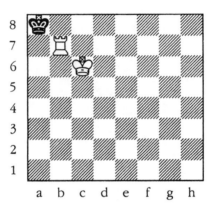

This is another case in which a player cannot benefit from material advantage. Black has no legal move, so the result is a stalemate.

Black to move: stalemate

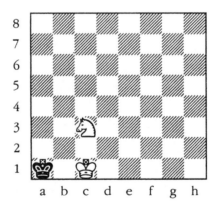

Knight and king against lone king is always a draw, with no checkmating possible. As here, the likely outcome is stalemate.

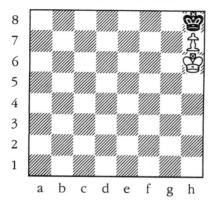

King and pawn against lone king is a common endgame and can produce checkmate, but the endgame must be correctly played. If Black is allowed to get his king to the promotion square (i.e., the square on which the advancing pawn would become a queen), a lone defending king can always draw against king and a-pawn or king and h-pawn.

White to move: stalemate

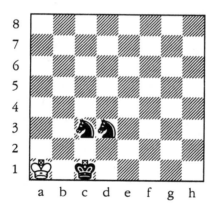

There are checkmate positions in the endgame of king and two knights versus lone king, but only if the defending side plays incorrectly. Here Black has hemmed in the white king so it cannot move. As a result, the position is a draw by stalemate. This is the best the stronger side can achieve, if the weaker side defends correctly.

FACING REALITY

If you absolutely cannot win, then go for a draw. A draw is always better than a defeat!

Occasionally, everyone—even Kasparov—loses. If you follow tournament play you will see that games are rarely played through to checkmate. Advanced players usually realize when defeat has become inevitable. All of which raises the question of:

When to resign?

Musashi was once asked to demonstrate his prowess at the court of the *shogun* by dueling against the most skilled Samurai from the Elite Bodyguard. Facing off with *shinai* (bamboo swords), the combatants launched simultaneous attacks. Their movements were like lightning, and as the outcome was unclear to those watching the swordsmen were asked to duel again. Once more the quickness of the action defied the senses. "It must be a draw," commented the shogun. "Yes, a draw," echoed Musashi's opponent proudly. "Doesn't anyone see what really happened?" protested Musashi. "There is no doubt of the outcome. If these swords were real, this man would be dead."

Indignant at Musashi's words, and filled with bravado, the bodyguard challenged: "Let's use real swords, then." Disinclined at this advanced stage of his career to take life, Musashi suggested that they break for tea, but the bodyguard was adamant. "Very well," said Musashi reluctantly. Once more the action took place in a flash. But this time the live blade told the true story. Musashi sustained a small cut on the lapel of his kimono, the bodyguard lay dying on the *tatami* floor, blood pouring through the massive gash in his chest. "What a waste," Musashi sighed.

In chess, the consequences of misjudging one's status are not quite so severe. In the film *Searching for Bobby Fischer*, based on the true life story of an American chess prodigy, the young Josh Waitzkin compassionately offers his opponent a draw in the deciding game of a championship match, even though he sees a forced mate in 12 moves. His adversary fails to see the inevitability of his own demise and declines, thus sealing his own fate.

Although fighting spirit and a never-say-die attitude are essential components of the champion's character, one should learn to recognize a truly hopeless situation and then resign gracefully. (Chess etiquette frowns on *seppuku* as too messy.) Of course, if even the faintest possibility remains, we recommend that you fight on to the bitter end. It is better to err on the side of resigning late than early; but when the game reaches a point at which defeat is mathematically certain, one should bow out, analyze and learn from mistakes, reset the pieces, and begin the next game.

BEATING TIME: PLAYING WITH THE CLOCK

Time controls were first introduced in 1861 for a match between the German master Adolf Anderssen (victor of the famous Immortal Game ten years previously, see page 184) and Baron Ignaz von Kolisch. Previously, the unlimited license granted to players to ponder moves had been open to abuse. The American Paul Morphy was driven almost to tears by the excessively slow play of Louis Paulsen, his German opponent, while Howard Staunton accused the notoriously slow-playing Elijah Williams of boring his opponents to death rather than outplaying them.

In all modern championship matches each player must complete a minimum of 40 moves in two hours. In speed chess all the moves must be completed in 30 minutes. In blitz chess, the whirlwind game played at Nintendo speed, the limit is five minutes — less time than it takes many players to contemplate a single move. Failure to complete the moves in the allotted time results in loss of the game by forfeit. In the eighth game of their World Championship match in London in 1986, Anatoly Karpov lost by time forfeit with no fewer than ten moves still to make against Garry Kasparov.

Pendulum clocks replaced early sand glasses in 1883. The push-button variety was introduced between 1895 and 1900. The modern tournament clock consists of two normal clock faces joined together. Each clock operates only when a button on the opposite clock is pushed downward. Players push their buttons—stopping their own clocks and starting their opponent's—as soon as they have completed their move. A small metal flag on each clock falls to signal the expiry of the player's allotted time.

Warfare and business operate under extreme pressure of time, while victory in martial arts often depends on split-second timing. Chess is no exception—and offers a marvelous training field for rapid decision-making.

9

THE WHITE BELT TESTS

We have now reached the stage at which you can take your Samurai Chess White Belt 6th and 5th Kyu tests. But before you do so, take time out to review the advice we give here.

THE GOLDEN RULES

Winning at chess means never losing sight of four sets of golden rules. All of these should now be familiar, since you have seen the examples of play in action.

The golden rule of the center

- Always try to occupy or control the center in some form.

The golden rule of mobilization

- Move your pawns immediately to powerful central positions — good opening moves are e2-e4 and . . . e7-e5 or d2-d4 and . . . d7-d5.

- Move out your bishops and knights quickly.
- Castle as soon as possible.

The golden rule of material

- Remember the relative values of the different pieces.
- Never forget that extra material almost always wins.
- Be constantly vigilant for threats to your pieces.
- Always capture enemy pieces when it is safe to do so.

The golden rule of checkmate

- Learn the Scholar's Mate and easy checkmating moves with king, queen, and rook.
- Remember that checkmating is always easier with material advantage.
- Look out for back-rank checkmates with rook or queen.

THE GOLDEN QUESTIONS

Before making a move, ask yourself these questions . . . EVERY TIME!
- Does my next move allow me to be checkmated?
- Can my next move checkmate my opponent?
- Can my next move win material?
- Does my next move lose material?

EXTRA MATERIAL USUALLY WINS

Napoleon said, "God is on the side of the big battalions!" Damon Runyon added, "The race is not always to the swift nor the fight to the strong, but that's the way to bet." In chess terms, *extra material usually wins*, and we do not hesitate to repeat this message.

Memorize the piece values:

Pawn   = 1
Knight   = 3
Bishop   = 3
Rook   = 5
Queen   = 9
King   is priceless

How good a player are you now? Are you ready to pass your first White Belt examination? We give you a chance to find out. Ultimately you will have the chance to test yourself in crucial positions from top players' games and to discover how your skill compares.

White Belt Test: 6th Kyu

Position 1

Black to play

Can the bishop capture the pawn?

Position 2

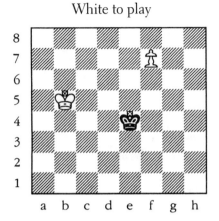

White to play

White can advance the pawn from f7 to f8. To which pieces can it promote?

Position 3

White to play

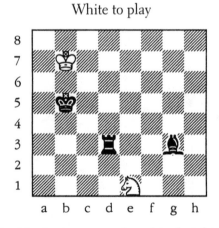

Which of the black pieces can the white knight capture?

Position 4

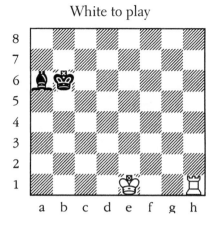

Neither the white king nor the white rook has moved so far. Can White castle?

Position 5

White to play

White to play. How many checkmates in one move are possible? Answers appear on page 117.

Once you have successfully tackled the 6th Kyu test, move on to the 5th Kyu test.

WHITE BELT TEST: 5TH KYU

Position 1

White to play

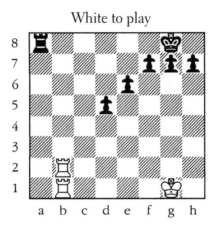

In this position Black has five pawns for a white rook, a full material equivalent. However, White can checkmate Black in two moves. How is this done?

Position 2

White to play

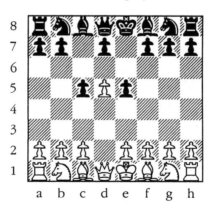

The opening moves of this game have been

1	d2-d4	c7-c5
2	d4-d5	e7-e5

Can the white pawn on d5 capture any black pawn *en passant?*

Position 3

White to play

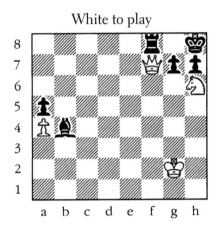

In this position it looks as if White must move the attacked queen, when Black will capture the knight and it will be difficult for White to win. However, White has a very clever checkmating idea leading to a devastating blow with the knight. Can you see it?

Position 4

White to play

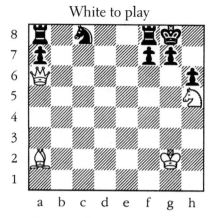

Here White, to play, can force a quick checkmate by utilizing the motif of the pin. How is this done?

Position 5

White to play

White has the black king trapped and can check endlessly with his rooks. However, the question is how to force a quick checkmate.

Answers are on pages 117 through 118.

White Belt Test: 6th Kyu—Answers

1. Yes. 1 . . . ♗a1xg7 is a legal move.
2. The white pawn can promote to queen, rook, bishop, or knight by advancing to f8. It cannot promote to a king, and if it moves to f8 it cannot stay on the board as a pawn.
3. The knight can capture the rook on d3, but not the bishop on g3.
4. White cannot castle because the black bishop on a6 controls the f1 square over which the white king would have to move. You cannot castle through check.
5. There are four mates in one: ♕a2-a1, ♕a2-b1, ♕a2-g2, and ♕a2-h2. Note the enormous versatility of the queen in giving checkmate from different directions.

White Belt Test: 5th Kyu—Answers

1. White forces checkmate in two moves by exploiting the imprisonment of the black king on the back rank, namely:

    1   ♖b2-b8+   ♖a8xb8
    2   ♖b1xb8 mate

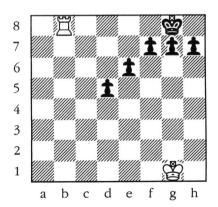

2. In this position White can play 3 d5xe6 *en passant* since Black's last move was . . . e7-e5. White cannot play 3 d5xc6 *en passant*, one reason being that the white pawn arrived on d5 after Black had played c7-c5.

3. White has an ingenious checkmate using the knight by means of 1 ♕f7-g8+ ♖f8xg8 and now the strike 2 ♘h6-f7 checkmate.

4. White wins by playing 1 ♕a6-g6 with the deadly threat of 2 ♕g6xg7 checkmate. The white queen can move right up close to the black king since the white bishop on a2 pins the f7-pawn to the black king and prevents Black's f-pawn capturing White's queen on g6.

5. The answer to this puzzle, which often annoys and frustrates inexperienced players, is that the white rooks must gain a maximum distance from the black king. Hence the solution is not to give any check with either rook, but 1 ♖d7-a7 ♔e8-d8. Now White has a choice of checkmates, either with 2 ♖a7-a8 or with 2 ♖f7-f8.

If you skipped any of the tests through inexperience of the workings of chess notation or of the pieces, now is the time to go back.

PART III

TRAINING FOR
MENTAL COMBAT

10

PERFECTING MIND AND BODY

Two samurai stand facing each other on the top of a mountain, their razor-sharp blades glistening in the morning sun. Each waits with perfect concentration for the slightest opening in his opponent's guard: a nanosecond lapse of concentration invites instant death.

At its highest level, the game of chess is similar. Only the fit and the brave can hope to survive a Grandmaster tournament. Genius is a useful asset but, as many talented players have discovered to their cost, by itself it is not enough. Vast reserves of physical and mental stamina are needed, plus psychological toughness, unbreakable concentration, and the kind of confidence that flirts with arrogance. These qualities are increasingly valuable to anyone aspiring to excellence in chess, martial arts, business—and life.

Before we explore (in Part Four) the seven essential principles of Samurai strategy and their application to chess, we want to introduce a mind-body program to prepare you to be a successful mental warrior. This is new and revolutionary material for anyone who wants to shine in competitive tournament chess at any level, including even Grandmasters!

THE POWER OF PRACTICE: PASSION OF THE GRANDMASTERS

In the martial arts, intense training regimens evolved as a matter of life or death. Every great master is characterized by religious devotion to training. Yamaoka Tesshu, the legendary Samurai swordmaster (see pages 33–35), led his senior students through a thousand days of continuous training followed by a day of *seigan* (vow). Participants in the *seigan* faced two hundred opponents in succession, with only the briefest period of rest. Graduates of this ordeal were invited to advanced training capped off by a second *seigan,* this time involving six hundred contests over three days. Survivors of the second *seigan* faced the ultimate challenge: seven days, fighting 1,400 opponents in succession.

In a chess parallel, co-author Raymond Keene once faced 107 opponents at one and the same time. In three and a half hours he won 101 games, drew five, and lost one.

Tesshu stated that he created this extraordinary trial because he was concerned that swordsmanship was becoming "a mere pastime with no bearing on matters of importance." He urged his students to

> strive with your entire being. Forcefully and without restraint, swing the sword over and over. Extend yourself to the fullest, and concentrate on executing the techniques naturally. Eventually, real strength will be fostered; all stiffness will vanish and the techniques can be performed in a free-flowing manner. The opponent's movement can be detected before he strikes—one intuitively knows where to cut and any attack can be repelled . . . train harder and harder!

Gichin Funakoshi, the legendary karate master, trained daily until his death at the age of ninety. His first rule for the study of karate ran:

> You must be deadly serious in training. When I say that, I do not mean that you should be reasonably diligent or moderately in earnest. I mean that your opponent must always be present in your mind, whether you sit or stand or walk or raise your arms.

Already long established as Japan's supreme martial artist, Morihei Ueshiba remarked, just a few weeks before his death, that "this old man must still train and train." For the greatest masters, training is not done merely to achieve a result in a contest; it becomes an end in itself, a way of life. The same is true for the great masters of chess.

The Grandmasters only play to the same rules, too, but they know them better than we do.

—Andreas Duckstein, International Master

The average chess master can play a simultaneous display against a group of solid club players and win most of the games handily. A strong Grandmaster can do the same with a group of masters. This phenomenon fascinated Adriaan de Groot, a Dutch psychologist. He wanted to know why Grandmasters were so much better than masters. Did they have higher IQs? Were Grandmasters endowed with superior memory or mathematical ability? In his classic study, *Thought and Choice in Chess*, published in 1965, de Groot demonstrated that the difference between masters and Grandmasters cannot be traced to any disparity in intellectual endowment. The distinguishing characteristic of Grandmasters is their love of the game. They play, practice, and think about chess more frequently, and are more passionately involved in it, than the masters.

We are told that talent creates its own opportunities. Yet, it sometimes seems that intense desire creates not only its own opportunities, but its own talents as well.

—Bruce Lee, *Tao of Jeet Kune Do*

Exhaustive preparation is an integral part of modern tournament play. With hundreds of competitions at the national and international level every year, the standard of knowledge, and the rate at which that knowledge is being acquired, is increasing dramatically. Analytical investigations of key lines in modern openings are published in an unstemmable flow of books, magazines, and computer-based data archives. No fully equipped modern Grandmaster would arrive at an important competition without his portable computer and chess database of many thousands of tactically important games.

This massive flow of up-to-the-minute information has led to in-depth research into certain opening variations, and also into the openings favored by specific players. Most modern Grandmasters have an astronomical knowledge of openings. It can even happen that, in effect, a player wins a game on prematch analysis alone, without departing from the basic patterns that might already have been worked out at home. Precisely this occurred in the tenth game of the 1995 World Championship in New York where Garry Kasparov reduced Viswanathan Anand's position to rubble with moves that Kasparov had worked out in advance, before the game started.

Originally the standard Japanese martial arts uniform (*gi*) came with a white belt (*obi*). The tradition of the "black belt" derives from the effects of constant practice on the *obi*—over the years it turned black from wear.

So, practice, practice, practice. Play at every opportunity, take a portable chess computer with you on trips, and read the daily chess column in *The Times* without fail. Memorizing openings and main lines of play and in-depth analysis of your games will form the backbone of your success. It is also especially valuable to study and memorize the games of the great champions. As you play and replay their classic contests you train yourself to think in a more expansive manner. Remember Musashi's words on the importance of strategy.

> Of course you cannot assemble a thousand or ten thousand men for everyday training. But you can become a master of strategy by training alone with a sword, so that you can understand the enemy's stratagems, his strength and resources, and come to appreciate how to apply strategy to beat ten thousand enemies.
>
> Any man who wants to master the essence of my strategy must research diligently, training morning and evening. Thus can he polish his skill, become free from self, and realize extraordinary ability. He will come to possess miraculous power.
>
> This is the practical result of strategy.

KNOW THE ENEMY

When preparing for a particular match, you will want to follow the advice of the great Chinese general Sun Tzu, one of history's supreme strategists:

> If you know the enemy and know yourself, you need not fear the result of a hundred battles. If you know yourself, but not the enemy, for every victory you will also suffer a defeat. If you know neither the enemy, nor yourself, you will succumb in every battle.

Sun Tzu also wrote: "What enables the wise sovereign and the good general to strike and conquer, and achieve things beyond the reach of ordinary men, is foreknowledge."

Chess masters have played a key role in "intelligence" work throughout the ages. Among the best-known are Sir Stuart Milner-Barry, Harry Golombek OBE (both former chess columnists of *The Times*) and C. H. O'D. Alexander CBE, who were instrumental in cracking German codes during World War II. The talent for chess common to all three made them particularly expert in the manipulation of complex series of letters and numbers. Indeed it was Sir Stuart Milner-Barry who personally delivered a plea to Sir Winston Churchill to increase funding for the chess section at their top-secret headquarters at Bletchley Park.

Foreknowledge, also known as "intelligence," is a critical element in determining the outcome of a conflict, whether between armies, businesses, or individuals. In Samurai times, each *ryu* kept detailed dossiers on their opponents' strategies and tactics. The difference between life and death was knowing which attacking style an enemy preferred, and so the Samurai took intelligence gathering very seriously. Chess players must do the same.

So learn all you can about your opponent's strengths and weaknesses. What openings does he prefer? How aggressive is he? How well does he manage the clock? Remember the words of Bruce Lee: "Half the battle is won when one knows what the adversary is doing." "To attack, you must study the adversary's weaknesses and strengths and take advantage of the former while avoiding the latter."

An example comes from the cutting edge of Man versus Machine chess contests.

After his clear but narrow victory over Deep Blue, Kasparov said: "Against a machine strategical psychology is very important. In certain positions, generally open positions, computer programs can be unbelievably strong. But they are also very weak in positions where they cannot see a plan. To play a machine, you have to limit its unlimited potential to find combinations and to threaten your king or other pieces. I tried to select the openings where the machine didn't have a clear plan."

Computer strengths and weaknesses:
The Kasparov vs. Deep Blue Matches

In spring 1996, Garry Kasparov was challenged by IBM's Deep Blue computer, the new incarnation of Deep Thought. The match was to be of six games with a $500,000 prize fund. Deep Blue could calculate 500 million different positions per second, and many computer experts predicted that this time the human World Champion would go down to defeat. The match aroused intense interest, including an eight-page feature in *Time* magazine and five million accesses on the World Wide Web site, a world record at the time, surpassed only by the ten million achieved for the Atlanta Olympics. By its own admission, IBM gained $200 million worth of world wide publicity for the contest.

Kasparov started the match in mistaken fashion. His strategy was to treat the machine as he would any human opponent and overwhelm it by brutal tactics. Unfortunately for Kasparov, Deep Blue's phenomenal calculating ability rendered this option more

Garry Kasparov, the human champion, prepares to outwit Deep Blue, IBM's silicon monster.

or less a nonstarter, and Kasparov succumbed in flames in the very opening game.

As the match wore on, Kasparov realized that the correct strategy was to deprive IBM's monster machine of opportunities for precise calculation. Kasparov spun a nebulous strategic web, imperceptibly stifling the machine's options and ultimately strangling it to death. The concluding position of the sixth game was particularly spectacular, with the computer's forces paralyzed in spite of its extra pawn.

Overall, Kasparov emerged the winner by 4 points to 2. He had learned the secrets of computer-hostile play: avoid premature sacrifices and hurried attacks; steal a square here, a small strategic advantage there; and gradually pile on the pressure.

The sense of relief in the media when Kasparov had finally defeated Deep Blue was palpable. *The Times* ran a typical headline: "IBM bows to champion who saved dignity of human race."

The final score in the six games was below:

	1	*2*	*3*	*4*	*5*	*6*	*Total*
Kasparov	0	1	½	½	1	1	4
Deep Blue	1	0	½	½	0	0	2

White: Kasparov; Black: Deep Blue
Challenge Match, Philadelphia 1996, Game 6
Queen's Gambit Declined, Slav Defense

Having so far used Simplified Modern Notation to assist inexperienced players, we now switch to the shortened version, which is standard in all chess books and newspaper chess columns. The main difference is that the shortened version does not (except in cases where two pieces of the same type can reach an identical square) specify the square from which a piece moves, only the square on which it lands.

1	♞f3	d5
2	d4	c6
3	c4	e6

| 4 | ♘bd2 | ♞f6 |
| 5 | e3 | c5 |

The computer strives for an open position, even at the cost of a tempo, but, having learned his lesson from an earlier defeat, Kasparov now plays resolutely to maintain a solid wall of pawns in the center.

6	b3	♞c6
7	♗b2	cxd4
8	exd4	♝e7
9	♖c1	0-0
10	♗d3	♝d7

This normal developing move proves strategically inadequate. More farsighted would be 10 . . . b6, planning to deploy the bishop on b7. After 10 . . . b6 11 cxd5 is met by 11 . . . ♞b4 when Black has an excellent position.

| 11 | 0-0 | ♞h5 |

A decentralizing maneuver, ultimately resulting in the loss of further time. Better would be 11 . . . ♖c8.

12	♖e1	♞f4
13	♗b1	♝d6
14	g3	♞g6
15	♞e5	.

This occupation of the center confirms White's initiative.

| 15 | . . . | ♖c8 |
| 16 | ♞xd7 | |

Sensibly securing the permanent advantage of the pair of bishops.

16	. . .	♛xd7
17	♞f3	♝b4
18	♖e3	♖fd8
19	h4	

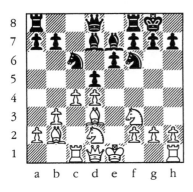

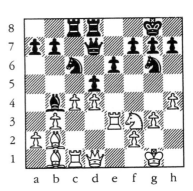

The next phase of the game is characterized by a steady advance of White's pawns on both flanks, driving back Black's pieces and swiftly securing a decisive advantage in terms of spatial control.

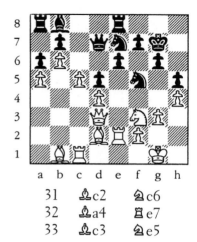

19	...	♘ge7
20	a3	♗a5
21	b4	♗c7
22	c5	♖e8
23	♕d3	g6
24	♖e2	♘f5
25	♗c3	h5
26	b5	♘ce7
27	♗d2	♔g7
28	a4	♖a8
29	a5	a6
30	b6	♗b8

White has advanced remorselessly on the queenside and Black's position is now desperate, with his remaining bishop and queen's rook virtually locked out of play and having no hope of attaining freedom.

31	♗c2	♘c6
32	♗a4	♖e7
33	♗c3	♘e5

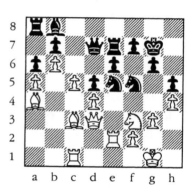

The computer tries its sole tactical trick of the game, designed to alleviate the annoying pin against its knight. If anything, this makes matters worse, since White can now establish a complete blockade.

34	dxe5	♕xa4
35	♘d4	♘xd4
36	♕xd4	♕d7
37	♗d2	♖e8
38	♗g5	♖c8
39	♗f6+	♔h7
40	c6	

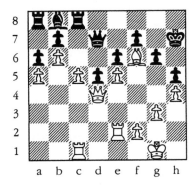

A fine sacrifice that either creates a deadly passed pawn (as

happens) or permits White to seize decisive control of the c-file after 40 . . . ♖xc6 41 ♖ec2.

40	. . .	bxc6
41	♕c5	♔h6
42	♖b2	♕b7
43	♖b4	Black resigns

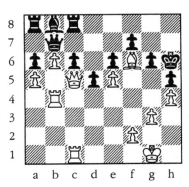

The utter strangulation inflicted on the black position recalls games by Dr. Tarrasch, the great nineteenth-century chess strategist. (Tarrasch was famous for gaining space advantage, usually with his pawns, and then throttling the opposition with a piece onslaught.) The computer has completely run out of sensible moves and can only shuffle its king backward and forward. A sample variation would be 43 . . . ♔h7 44 ♔g2 ♔h6 45 f4 ♔h7 46 ♕e7 ♕xe7 47 ♗xe7 ♖e8 48 ♗c5 when the threat of b7 is decisive.

Kasparov played this game very well, succeeding in keeping Deep Blue's awesome tactical skill at bay and providing a textbook demonstration of the art of playing against machines. It repays study by players keen to get the better of their home computer.

In switching from tactics to strategy, Kasparov did exactly what Musashi advised:

> The "mountain-sea" spirit means that it is bad to repeat the same thing several times when fighting the enemy. There may be no help but to do something twice, but do not try it a third time. If you once make an attack and fail, there is little chance of success if you use the same approach again. If you attempt a technique which you have previously tried unsuccessfully and fail yet again, then you must change your attacking method.
>
> If the enemy thinks of the mountains, attack like the sea; and if he thinks of the sea, attack like the mountains. You must research this deeply.

May 1997 brought a fresh challenge by Deep Blue to Kasparov's supremacy. The machine's analytical ability had been more than doubled as, indeed, had the prize fund put up by IBM, which now stood at $1.1 million.

This time the computer triumphed, 3.5 points to 2.5, in a match that broke many records. In the final hour of play alone, 22 million internet hits were registered to follow the moves of the game, 12 million more than for the entire three weeks of the 1996 Atlanta Olympics. Experts estimated that IBM had achieved 200 million dollars' worth of international publicity for a total prize fund outlay of a mere 1.1 million dollars. Even senior officers of Bill Gates's Microsoft Corporation took their hats off in public at IBM's achievement. It was a PR coup of staggering dimension.

Here is the final game of the match that allowed the computer to win by a one-point margin.

In October 1996 at Jena in Germany, grandmaster Gennadi Timoshenko, formerly Garry Kasparov's second, contested a match against a combination of the Fritz computer program and human minder called Ingo Althöfer. The match was ultimately won by the symbiotic Fritz/Althöfer tandem by 4½ to 3½. In one game of this match, Timoshenko risked exactly the same variation, as Black, with which Kasparov suffered such a debacle in the following game.

In the *International Computer Chess Association Journal* of

March 1997, Timoshenko published his game and his detailed conclusions on the sacrifice, which included the verdict: "After the knight sacrifice, Black has enough possibilities for defense." It is surprising that Kasparov's preparation should have overlooked Timoshenko's conclusion in this prime source for information on computer advances.

Deep Blue–Kasparov
New York, May 1997
Caro-Kann Defense

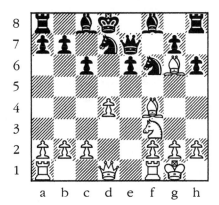

1 e4 c6 d4 d5 3 Nc3 dxe4 4 Nxe4 Nd7 5 Ng5 Ngf6 6 Bd3 e6 7 N1f3 h6 8 Nxe6

Timoshenko writes that Black's position after 7 . . . h6, contrary to the initial reaction of all the experts, present company included, is, in fact, defensible for Black. The problems came later. **8 . . . Qe7 9 0-0 fxe6 10 Bg6+ Kd8 11 Bf4**(diagram) This is the critical moment. Here Fritz/Althöfer-Timoshenko, Jena 1996 continued **11 . . . Nd5 12 Bg3 Qb4 13 Qb1 Ne7 14 c3 Qa5 15 Bh4 Kc7 16 Bg3+ Kd8 17 Bh4 Kc7** with equality. **11 . . . b5 12 a4** After Black's error on the previous move his position now falls apart. **12 . . . Bb7 13 Re1 Nd5 14 Bg3 Kc8 15 axb5 cxb5 16 Qd3 Bc6 17 Bf5 exf5 18 Rxe7 Bxe7 19 c4** Black resigns **19 . . . bxc4 20 Qxc4 Bb7 21 Qa6 checkmate** or **19 . . . Nb4 20 Bxf5 bxc4 21 Ne5**

Rd8 22 Nxc6 Nxc6 23 Bf4 with decisive gains. Having praised Kasparov for his insight into his opponent's playing methods after his victory in the 1996 match, this revenge game by the computer is a frightful warning as to what can occur if a player, even the greatest, loses track of the way in which his opponent truly operates.

If Kasparov had noticed the *ICCA* article, it might have changed the course of chess history.

In the wake of its victory, IBM announced that Deep Blue has retired from chess, turning down Kasparov's request for a third match. The machine will not be hanging up its pieces and munching chips on a beach; instead it has been assigned to new number-crunching duties, analyzing data on finance, investment, and medicine. "We've climbed Mount Everest, and now it's time to move on" was the final reaction of an IBM spokesperson.

Nevertheless, the chess community will not be convinced that IBM has finally triumphed over the human chess mind. The margin of victory was minimal, and six games is a decidedly small sample on which to base any far-reaching assessment.

Kasparov, as might be expected, was furious, saying: "I am very disappointed at IBM's statement. From the beginning, I believed in this concept as a scientific experiment coupled with a way of bringing chess into almost every home in the world. I am amazed to read that they wish 'to quit while they are ahead.' We stand at one match all and there is enormous worldwide enthusiasm for a tie-breaking third match. This action has the appearance of an investor cashing in their chips on the stock market—take your profits and run. It puts a lie to the scientific experiment and good-of-mankind theory they have espoused."

DEVELOPING INTUITION AND CREATIVITY

In modern elite chess competition, "foreknowledge" of your opponent's tendencies and a vast knowledge of openings and Grandmaster games are just the beginning. You must also cultivate creativity and intuition. Mikhail Tal, World Champion in 1960–61, emphasized: "A great many people have mastered the multiplication tables of chess nowadays and even know its logarithm tables by heart—therefore an attempt should occasionally be made to prove that two times two can also make five."

The whole philosophy of chess has changed. Early in the century the game's leading practitioners paid little attention to openings, and built their strategies on a platform of sound defense. Today, in the age of information technology, the game is necessarily more dynamic. Instead of relying on fundamental rules accessible to everyone, top players seek out the exceptions to the rules.

Bruce Lee: "Set patterns, incapable of adaptability, of pliability, only offer a better cage."

—*Tao of Jeet Kune Do*

Musashi: "A swordsman should not have a favorite sword."

—*A Book of Five Rings*

Do not become too attached to a favorite opening or style of play. Play what you need in order to win.

In all the following positions, the unsuspecting opponent was totally poleaxed by a surprise, way-out-of-the-ordinary strike.

The four positions witness play by some of the all-time greats. Mikhail Botvinnik was World Champion from 1948 to 1963, with a couple of breaks, and was essentially of the scientific Soviet school of chess. Tigran Petrosian was the man who ultimately dethroned Botvinnik, while the genius of American chess is represented by Paul Morphy and Bobby Fischer. Even the victims are illustrious. For example, for three decades Paul Keres was recognized as being one of the world's top three players, so defeating him was obviously no pushover.

White: Botvinnik; Black: Keres
USSR Team Championship 1966

In this seemingly complex situation, in which both sides have attacks in train and where both kings seem somewhat exposed, Botvinnik suddenly brought down the curtain with 1 ♖b8!! After this coup, Black resigned, since his queen had been wrenched by force from its defense of the pawn on h4. After, for example, 1 . . . ♛xb8 2 ♕xh4 Black has no defense to mate starting with ♕h7.

White to play

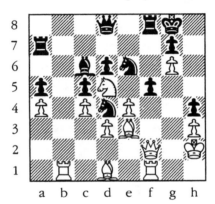

White: Keres; Black: Petrosian
World Championship Qualifier 1959

Tigran "The Tiger" Petrosian, a future World Champion, has sacrificed a rook for the attack. He must act at once, or he will succumb to White's superior force: a sensational finale.

Black to play

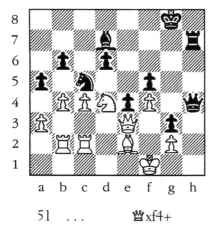

51 ...   ♛xf4+

White resigns on account of 52 ♛xf4 ♜h1 mate.

White: Morphy;
Black: The Duke of Brunswick and Count Isouard
Paris 1858

A spectacular checkmate, a queen and a knight down.

White to play

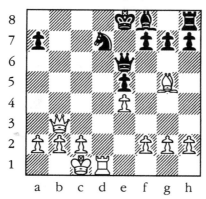

White wins with:

1	♕b8+!!	♘xb8
2	♖d8	checkmate

White: Robert Byrne; Black: Bobby Fischer
U.S. Championship 1964

Black to play

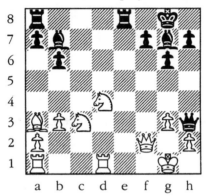

Showing his killer instinct, Fischer won this U.S. Championship with a 100 percent score. With Black to move, several Grandmasters were predicting a Fischer loss since he is a piece for a pawn down, but he revealed the astounding win:

1	...	♖e1+
2	♖xe1	♗xd4
3	♕xd4	♕g2
	checkmate	

There was an elite band of assassins in old Japan called the Ninja. They would plot and scheme, for years if necessary, to enter an enemy stronghold and the incredible variety of ways they discovered, to scale castle walls, or to remain undetected, gave the impression that they could fly or disappear at will. They were also masters of disguise and would circulate among the enemy, spreading rumors about their own fantastic exploits. They would strike only when fear had been sown and on moonless nights in the foulest of weather—then disappear again, along a route prepared months in advance, with traps for pursuing soldiers. Yet their terrifying abilities were really no more than techniques—tesujis—learned through constant practice and passed on from father to son. Every Shogi player should be something of a ninja and take a pride in perfecting his techniques of gaining access to the enemy stronghold and then delivering the mortal blow.

—John Fairbairn, *Guide to Shogi*.
Shogi is the Japanese form of chess.

11

GAMESMANSHIP: WINNING THROUGH INTIMIDATION

A chess match is a war of attrition, and the struggle does not always confine itself to the movements on the board. Strategists seek advantages wherever they may be found. In kendo, for example, many *kata* begin with a move known as *asahi*, "the rising sun." The sword is drawn and raised, and the blade is rotated so that it catches the sun's rays and reflects them into the eyes of the opponent. When he blinks, the swordsman surges forward and cuts him down. One of the earliest chess theorists, a sixteenth-century Spanish priest named Ruy Lopez, suggested so arranging the pieces and board before the game that the sunlight shines into the opponent's eyes.

Mikhail Botvinnik, the father of the modern Soviet dynasty, who became World Champion in 1948, greatly influenced the trend to prematch preparation. His researches were so immense, and his training sessions so thorough, that, detesting tobacco, he acclimatized himself in training games by encouraging opponents to blow smoke into his eyes. (Smoking is now banned during tournaments.) He relinquished the title for the last time in 1963, when he lost to Tigran Petrosian, the wily Armenian.

Gamesmanship, or psychological warfare, first became a major factor in the World Championship match between Boris Spassky, Petrosian's conqueror, and Bobby Fischer in Reykjavik in 1972. In an atmosphere heightened by political as much as by sporting tension, Fischer demanded exclusive use of his hotel swimming pool and insisted that the size of the official chessboard should be reduced by 3 millimeters. In retaliation the Soviet delegation alleged that electronic or chemical equipment was distracting Spassky, and demanded a search of the playing hall, including an X-ray examination of the players' chairs. The sum total of the search was two dead flies.

When Fischer surrendered the championship by default, the title was awarded to Anatoly Karpov, the brilliant young Russian. But the return of the championship behind the Iron Curtain did not bring the end of political intrigue. It has been suggested that, in his later matches with Garry Kasparov, Karpov had the benefit of a "dirty tricks" campaign conducted by the KGB.

Musashi focused on the environment in a part of his text titled "Depending on the Place":

> Stand in the sun; that is, take up an attitude with the sun behind you. If the situation does not allow this, you must try to keep the sun on your right side. In buildings, you must stand with the entrance behind you or to your right. Make sure that your rear is unobstructed, and that there is free space on your left, your right side being occupied with your sword attitude. At night, if the enemy can be seen, keep the fire behind you and the entrance to your right, and otherwise take up your attitude as above. You must look down on the enemy, and take up your attitude on slightly higher places.

Even though most modern tournaments are held indoors, glaring examples of gamesmanship can be seen regularly. Your good breeding may lead you to reject these ploys, but at the very least you must be prepared when an opponent springs one on you.

Remember Musashi's words: "In duels of strategy you must move the opponent's attitude. Attack where his spirit is lax, throw him into confusion, irritate and terrify him. Take advantage of the enemy's rhythm when he is unsettled and you can win."

CLOCK ANTICS

The introduction of a physical element—the clock—into an ostensibly intellectual activity is itself enough to disconcert some players. Common diversionary practices at battle-of-nerves time include panic-stricken staring at the clock face, bouncing up and down in the chair, and thumping the clock when a move is made. Several Grandmasters—Henrique Mecking, Walter Browne, and Viktor Korchnoi among them—indulge in exaggeratedly nerve-racking demonstrations during time trouble, which can have the effect of screwing up the tension and unsettling their opponents. Mecking, the Brazilian Grandmaster, was famous for holding down his hand so firmly during time scrambles that his opponent could not press the clock. Not to be outdone, Florin Gheorghiu, Romania's Grandmaster, executes baroque flourishes with his pieces when under pressure, brandishing them in the air before crashing them onto the board. Raymond Keene once saw him hurl a rook so savagely that it ricocheted off the board and hit his opponent on the head!

PARAPSYCHOLOGISTS, HYPNOTISTS, AND MYSTICS

The most extreme example of gamesmanship in a World Championship match occurred in the clash in the Philippines at Baguio City in 1978, between Anatoly Karpov, the golden boy of the Soviet establishment, holder of the Order of Lenin and World Chess Champion, and Viktor Korchnoi, the Soviet defector and general bad boy of international chess, whom the press in the Philippines nicknamed the Leningrad Lip.

In this protracted match of 32 games, the players hated each other so much that it proved impossible to "bury the hatchet," so frozen had the metaphorical ground between them become. Both sides employed merciless intimidation techniques. Karpov hired a so-called parapsychologist to sit in the front row of the auditorium and beam mind-bending rays at Korchnoi, or so Korchnoi claimed, while Korchnoi engaged orange-clad mystic gurus from the banned Ananda Marga sect to levitate for victory for him and conduct regular morning chanting sessions. The sect members were on bail for attempted murder, which did not ease matters.

In the battle between astral gurus and crazed parapsychologists, parapsychology ultimately won by six to five with 21 draws, and Karpov remained champion.

The Staredown

In competitive martial arts the "staredown" has become almost *de rigueur.* Perhaps the greatest master was Muhammad Ali, the former heavyweight boxing champion, whose stare seemed to suck the life from his victims. In chess, World Champion Mikhail Tal cultivated a penetrating stare that many of his adversaries found extremely disconcerting. One of them, Grandmaster Pal Benko, tried to ward off the effects of Tal's "evil eye" by wearing dark glasses during play.

While attacking, you should look as boldly aggressive as a beast of prey—without becoming reckless—in order to bring pressure at once upon the adversary's morale.

—Bruce Lee, *Tao of Jeet Kune Do*

The most intimidating player in chess history also happens to be the best: Garry Kasparov. Fred Waitzkin describes Kasparov's presence at a simultaneous exhibition in France:

Kasparov moved swiftly from board to board as if someone were pacing him in a race, pushing pawns and pieces ahead. He is beautiful when he plays, a wild creature. His body is tense, his face taut, punishing, at times fierce, as if he is about to physically attack. I have seen top Grandmasters wither from his fury, becoming disheveled, alarmed (although others are caught in the jet stream of his energy and genius and play their inspired best against him). He paused at one board, his bottom lip stuck out, mirroring an inner churning.

As he thought, there was a sway to his body, a connection between the mind that created games brimming with complexity so deep that few in the world could fully understand them, and the long graceful sweep of his arm moving a bishop across a diagonal, the athletic move from board to board. Indeed, he said later, he is a rhythm player, making better and better moves when he is on the beat from game to game. . . .

Kasparov's intimidating physical presence at the board set him apart from the other Grandmasters here. Confronted by his glowering look, an opponent lost confidence in his own ideas.

THE WINNING ATTITUDE

Beyond the staredown, true masters of the martial arts possess an overwhelming presence that defeats would-be opponents before the first blow is delivered. This confident radiance is effortless and unselfconscious, a result of decades of training mind, body, and spirit.

Before the struggle, victory is mine.

—Aikido Shihan, Mitsugi Saotome

Great things are to be won by resolute self-confidence and daring.

—Emanuel Lasker, World Champion for almost 27 years

One of the secrets of this indomitable confidence is to overcome the fear of death. For chess players the equivalent is to overcome the fear of losing. All the top players we know have a profound desire to win, and they hate to lose. But hating and fearing are different, and the distinction is critical. Hating to lose keeps you focused, fear of loss is distracting.

The Samurai approach to chess urges you to let go of the fear of losing and concentrate on playing your best. Cultivate a Zen-like detachment from the ego, focusing attention purely on the best possible moves. Musashi wrote: "Generally speaking, the Way of the warrior is resolute acceptance of death."

It is possible to misinterpret this as an exhortation to run berserk risks. On the chessboard this can be fatal. Musashi's advice is not intended to lure either the Samurai warrior or the chess player into insane folly in search of victory at all costs, but to suppress thoughts of victory and defeat while playing and to subordinate such desires to finding the best possible solution at every stage. It is difficult to achieve this attitude of mind, but it is well worth cultivating.

LEARN FROM EVERY LOSS

The legendary karate Grandmaster Suzuki Sensei was fighting a particularly challenging opponent in the Japanese National Championship competition. Suzuki was so good that his opponent's only hope was to launch an all-out attack. Amazingly, the challenger penetrated Suzuki's perimeter and landed a solid *mai geri* (front snap kick) squarely to the master's most vulnerable area. Staggered, Suzuki stood unconscious for a moment and then began to fall. As his balance left him his consciousness returned. His response was extraordinary: In his own words, "Thinking . . . falling. If falling . . . losing. Thinking . . . standing!" With tremendous will, Suzuki regained his balance and knocked his attacker out with one devastating counterpunch.

One of the real tests of a champion in any discipline is the ability to recover quickly and effectively from mistakes. Whatever your level, you will sometimes make blunders and mistakes. And everyone loses from time to time. But those who succeed in the long term—in martial arts, chess, business, and life—cultivate the ability to recover quickly from errors and to learn from their defeats.

Whoever moves his hand and does not draw back is a great man.

—Inscription on many Chinese chessboards

Aron Nimzowitsch, author of *My System,* wrote his masterwork as a result of his in-depth analysis of a series of defeats at the hands of players he thought he should beat. Here is an example.

White: Nimzowitsch; Black: Fluss
Zürich 1906

In this position, it is true, White can capture the black knight and thus win a piece. However, that is little consolation when faced by Black's massive threat of . . . ♖h6 followed by . . . ♕xh2+ and imminent checkmate.

White to play

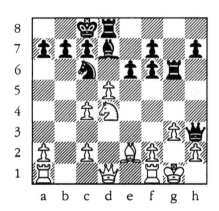

In this seemingly hopeless situation, Nimzowitsch played

1   dxc6   ♗xc6

Now Black not only threatens . . . ♖h6, but also . . . ♕g2 checkmate. To make matters worse, the black rook on d8 pins White's knight on d4 to the white queen so 2 ♘f3 is not a good defense. Nevertheless, Nimzowitsch continued.

2   ♘xc6   ♖xd1
3   ♖xd1   bxc6

White to play

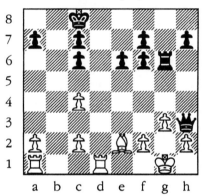

Here, Black has won White's queen and still has . . . ♖h6 in reserve. At this point Fluss leaned over to Nimzowitsch and asked him whether he would like to resign. Nimzowitsch's response was to play

4   c5

in his turn threatening 5 ♗a6+ ♔b8 6 ♖d8 checkmate. Therefore, Black had no choice; his rook had to retreat.

4   . . .   ♖g8

Now came the *coup de grâce*, which rocked Black out of his seat.

5   ♜b1

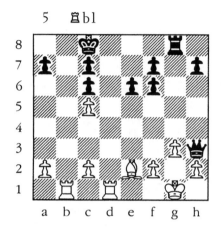

Suddenly, Black's king is trapped by the two white rooks and there is no defense to the threat of ♗a6 checkmate. Now it was Nimzowitsch's turn to smile at Fluss, but Fluss took the hint and resigned.

The next example of recovering balance comes from the London International of 1981, where co-author Raymond Keene won first prize, ahead of many Grandmasters and a former World Champion. White's pieces look aggressively positioned, but Black has set up an impenetrable defense, blocking White's options. Indeed, on closer inspection, it is White's position that is desperate. The reason is that Black's two knights and bishop combine in attack to doom White's pawn on c4. If Black wins the pawn, White's position will ultimately collapse. White's pawns on c3 and c4 are known as doubled pawns, and they can often be a source of possible weakness.

White: Keene; Black: Ligterink
London 1981

White to play

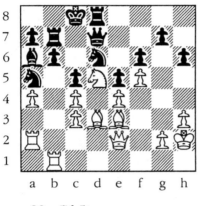

29   ♖b5!

An "exchange" offer (sacrifice of a rook for knight or bishop) to blunt Black's pressure against the c4-pawn. An added bonus is the opening of the a-file. This resolute action starts to turn the tables.

29   ...   ♗xb5

Black snatches the bait.

30	axb5	♔b8
31	♖a3	♖c8
32	♕a2	♕f7?

Black overlooks a fresh exchange sacrifice that disables his position. Correct is 32 ... ♕d8.

33   ♖xa5!

Another shock for Black.

33	...	bxa5
34	♕xa5	♕f8

There is no time to sit on this volcanic position. 34 . . . g6! is forced.

$$35 \quad \text{♛a6} \qquad \text{♞e8}$$

An improvement is 35 . . . ♖d7 36 ♛a3 ♞b7 37 ♗e2 ♛f7!, although at this point it is not so easy to grasp that ♗e2-h5 must be stopped.

$$36 \quad \text{♛a3} \qquad \text{♛d6}$$
$$37 \quad \text{♗e2!}$$

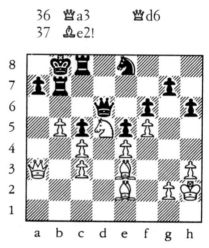

On material criteria alone Black is 28 points to 25 points ahead, and should win. But White's sacrifices have turned a static situation into a dynamic one, and have also unbalanced Black's mental equilibrium. Now the threat of ♗h5 suddenly leaves Black hamstrung. Ligterink decides to jettison excess baggage.

37	. . .	♔a8
38	♗h5	♞c7
39	♗xc5	♞xb5
40	♗xd6	♞xa3
41	♗xa3	♖xc4

After the game Ligterink preferred 41 . . . a5.

42	♗b4	♖xe4
43	♗f3	♖c4
44	♘e3	

The smoke has cleared—now White is playing for the win!

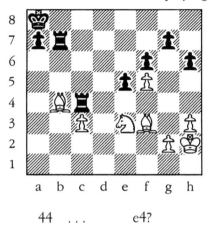

| 44 | ... | e4? |

A time-pressure error. Better is 44 ... ♖cc7, with drawing chances.

45	♘xc4	exf3
46	g4	♖d7
47	♔g3	♖d3
48	♔f2	♔b7
49	♘e3	♔b6

At last White can achieve a winning material advantage.

50	♔xf3	♔b5
51	♔e4	♖d7
52	♘c2	a5
53	♘d4+	♔b6
54	♗a3	a4
55	c4	Black resigns

The sudden turn of events left Black stunned. Ligterink could not cope with the rapid-fire changes from an apparent technical win to a running battle.

One of his students once asked Morihei Ueshiba, "How is it that you move with such total perfection, that you never make any mistakes?" Ueshiba smiled and replied, "Ah, I make mistakes all the time, I just correct them so quickly, that you can't see it."

FACING LESSER-RATED OR HIGHER-RATED OPPONENTS

As a martial artist, or a chess player, most of your contests will be against others of similar level. But you will occasionally face those of lower rank and, if you are lucky, you will find opponents with superior experience. Indeed, sparring with seniors is the secret of accelerating progress in the martial arts. What are the keys to facing opponents of differing rank, rating, or experience?

First, how to deal, in competition, with lesser opponents? In the *dojo*, rank beginners inflict many injuries and upsets on senior students. Overconfident, and therefore sloppy green, brown and sometimes even black belts make themselves vulnerable to the often awkward and "improper" attacks of neophytes. Similarly, in chess, less experienced players often ignore standard openings, launching unconventional assaults that, defying preparatory analysis, must be met with vigilance. Moreover, no matter how good you are, it is worth bearing in mind the old Japanese admonition, "Even monkeys fall out of trees"—even the best players make staggering blunders. So, never underestimate your opponent. Take no one lightly. Prepare for every game as though you were facing a rattlesnake.

Here is a fantastic example of a very big monkey falling out of an apparently very secure tree. It was played in the second round of the Amsterdam 1956 tournament between two contenders for the World Championship.

White: Petrosian; Black: Bronstein
World Championship Qualifier, Amsterdam 1956

White to play

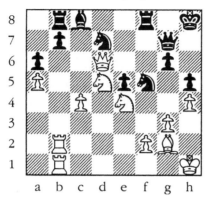

Here White's position is absolutely dominating, and if he now plays 1 ♕c7 Black's position is so disorganized and crushed that he will soon suffer heavy material losses. Instead, carried away by premature dreams of victory, Petrosian, who became World Champion seven years later, carelessly played 1 ♘g5??. In doing so he totally overlooked that Bronstein could respond with 1 . . . ♘xd6, winning White's queen for nothing and causing White to resign at once—a tragic lapse of concentration, certainly caused by a premature mental victory celebration.

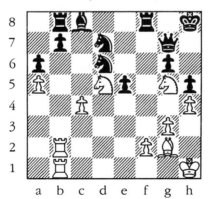

Second, how about facing someone of higher rank? What do you do if you are a brown belt facing a black belt? Or a chess player facing an opponent with a superior Elo rating? Let the following story be your inspiration.

Before his death in 1616 Tokugawa *shogun* Ieyasu signed an infamous decree, *Kirisute gomen* ("the right to cut down and leave"). This gave legal sanction to members of the Samurai class to bifurcate anyone who offended them immediately, for any reason, even a trifle, without consequence. One day, Seichi, a teacher of *chan-no-yu*, the Japanese Tea Ceremony, inadvertently offended a notoriously edgy high-ranking Samurai. Instead of cutting him down on the spot, the Samurai challenged Seichi to a duel at sunrise.

Although Seichi's study of the way of tea had taught him to access a deep inner calm, he was not a student of any martial art and had never before wielded a *katana*. He sought the counsel of a friend, the abbot of a nearby Zen monastery. The abbot motioned Seichi to enter the tearoom of the monastery, and asked him to lead the tea ceremony. When they finished, the Zen Master told him that his chances of surviving a duel with the Samurai were slim, but that he would die with honor if he approached combat with the same attitude he brought to the ritual of the tea ceremony. The Zen Master said: "Wield the sword straightforwardly, as you hold the ladle in the tea ceremony; and, applying the same precision and clarity of mind with which you pour the boiling water onto the tea, step forward, with no thought of the consequence, and strike through the center line of your opponent."

Seichi embraced his friend's counsel and cast off all fear, all thoughts of life or death. The next morning Seichi stood in meditation at the top of the hill where the duel was to take place. As the Samurai approached, he stopped, stunned and frozen by the cool serenity and radiant presence he had not expected to encounter. "Sumimasen" ("Excuse me"), "Gomen Nasai" ("I'm sorry"), said the Samurai, and bowed deeply before walking off into the still-rising sun.

Musashi wrote:

"To become the enemy" means to think yourself into the enemy's position. In the world people tend to think of a robber trapped in a house as a fortified enemy. However, if we think of "becoming the enemy," we feel that the whole world is against us and that there is no escape. He who is shut inside is a pheasant. He who enters is a hawk. You must appreciate this.

In a large-scale strategy, people are always under the impression that the enemy is strong, and so tend to become cautious. But if you have good soldiers, and if you understand the principles of strategy, and if you know how to beat the enemy, there is nothing to worry about.

In single combat also you must put yourself in the enemy's position. If you think, "Here is a master of the Way, who knows the principles of strategy," then you will surely lose. You must consider this deeply.

Playing mind sports offers a telescopic glimpse of a wider picture: it teaches things which people assume you can only learn after years of experience. People learn that concentration is crucial; that you can't get better at anything without hard work; that your memory really can improve; that you should never be complacent about your own abilities; that it is important to appear confident, even when you are not; that when all seems doomed, there is still a chance. . . .

—Paraphrased from *Punch* magazine, September 1996

12

HARMONIZING YOUR PHYSICAL AND MENTAL POWERS

Aerobic conditioning, weight training, stretching, and endless repetition of technique are the cornerstones of martial arts training. Martial artists aim to condition their physical reflexes for lightning response. Yet great masters emphasize that at the highest levels of combat the edge goes to the fighter with superior confidence and mental discipline. In the words of Morihei Ueshiba, "When surrounded by a forest of enemy spears, enter deeply and learn to use your mind as a shield." In *Zen and the Art of Archery*, Eugen Herrigel describes the legendary Master Awa urging him to "forget your physical strength and shoot only with your strength of mind."

While the mental discipline of chess is obvious, at the highest level of combat the edge may belong to the player with greater physical conditioning, stamina, and presence. Wilhelm Steinitz was the first great player to advocate the importance of regular exercise for training world-class chess competitors.

Superstar Bobby Fischer's preparations for World Championship matches included weight lifting, hitting the heavy bag, tennis, swimming, and healthy eating. In *Bobby Fischer: Profile of a Prodigy*, Fischer told Frank Brady, "You can't separate mind from body. . . . Your body has to be in top condition." World Champion Garry Kasparov, the player with the highest Elo rating of all time, is also a devotee of weight lifting, boxing, and aerobic conditioning.

World Chess Champion Garry Kasparov knows the importance of supreme physical fitness for his mental battles.

Appropriate fitness training is recommended for anyone who wishes to fulfill their intellectual potential. For the serious chess player it is essential.

Fitness for Mental Athletes

We present here a body/mind fitness regimen for mental athletes covering exercise, diet, meditation, poise, and a special program of warm-ups drawn from the martial arts for use before both martial arts and chess competitions.

Some 124 governments around the world officially recognize tournament chess as a sport. A recent study by Dr. Christian Hollinsky in Vienna, who subjected chessplayers under tournament conditions to physical and psychometric tests measuring heart rate, blood pressure and stress levels, indicates that chessplayers show greater signs of physical activity during a competition game than do competitors in many standard sports.

Dr. Hollinsky's study demonstrated that chessplayers in good physical condition, even those of advanced age, are better able to withstand the physical pressures of tournament chess. During a tournament game the heart rate of chessplayers is comparable to that of cyclists while adrenaline levels in chess can be even greater than those in both cycling and football.

—*The Times*, 1996

Aerobics

Dr. Kenneth Cooper, who originated aerobics, found that regular moderate exercise has profoundly beneficial effects on the body and the mind. Aerobic ("with oxygen") exercise strengthens the cardiovascular system, improving blood and therefore oxygen flow to the body and brain. On average the brain represents less than 3 percent of body weight, yet it uses more than 30 percent of the body's oxygen. As you become aerobically fit, you double your capacity to process oxygen.

Cooper and many others have demonstrated that a regular program of aerobic exercise leads to significant improvements in alertness, emotional stability, mental acuity, and stamina. It generally takes an "out-of-shape" individual six weeks, exercising for at least twenty minutes four times a week (and raising the heart rate to approximately 120 beats per minute), to produce marked benefits. (Consult your physician for guidance on beginning your own program.)

The secret to beginning a successful aerobic training program is to find activities that you enjoy. Brisk walking, running, dancing, swimming, rowing, or martial arts training can be combined to create your ideal program. Do this and your match and tournament chess results will inevitably improve!

Strength

Competitive martial artists know that weight training is an efficient method of developing strength, muscle tone, and the resilience of connective tissue and bone. It is also the most efficient method for burning unnecessary body fat. Physical strength and lively muscle tone support the capacity for focused attention and mental stamina. Thus weight lifting is invaluable for anyone seeking an advantage in chess and other mental sports. To begin your own strength-training program, find a good coach or trainer and seek guidance on developing proper form.

A *Times* reporter described Garry Kasparov training for the ultimate mental combat:

> Sweat streams off the Champion's face. Gobbets of it run out of his graying hair, slide down his temple, his cheeks, hang off his chin for a second, then soak into his darkening T-shirt. He's a very fit man, but this is a very tough work out. He has 90kg on the bar now: his own body weight plus about 20lb. If he lifts it, he will have set a new personal best. Garry Kasparov is flanked by Sacha and Eu-

gene, his two personal fitness trainers. Sacha and Eugene are also very fit and very big with it. Kasparov seizes the bar from its rest, steps back, grimaces, pounds the metal up above his head, locks his arms, locks his legs, flares his nostrils, inevitably succeeds, dumps the weight back down to the attendant heavies. Applause and flash bulbs fill the small gym as the crowd acknowledges the Champion's latest achievement. This is Kasparov in serious training. Championship chess is a grueling business and fitness will be important as he prepares for the two-million dollar showdown.

Flexibility

Every martial arts class begins with a series of stretching exercises. Besides preventing injury, stretching benefits your circulatory and immune systems. Practice simple stretching exercises before and after aerobic and strength training, upon getting up, and before every chess match. The secret to a good stretch is to take your time, bring your full awareness to the process, and allow easy release of muscle groups in harmony with extended exhalations. Never bounce or try to force a stretch.

Diet

Healthful eating habits will help you to maintain an even physiological and emotional keel throughout the day. Combined with aerobics, strength training, and flexibility exercises, a healthful diet will improve your ability to concentrate. Although diet fads come and go, the fundamental truths of intelligent eating stand the tests of time and scientific scrutiny. We summarize them here.

THE SAMURAI CHESS DIET

- **Seek fresh, wholesome food.** Avoid overprocessed, additive-injected "junk" foods.

- **Eat plenty of fiber.** Raw vegetables, bran, and other fiber-rich foods "brush" and exercise your digestive tract, keeping it active and healthy.
- **Avoid overeating.** Learn to stop eating just before you are full. You will feel better and probably live longer. (Experiments have shown that slightly underfed rats live twice as long as those that gorge themselves.) Eat lightly before playing so that your circulatory system can bring maximal oxygen to your brain rather than have to work primarily on your digestion.
- **Drink enough water.** Your body is 80 percent water and needs a regular supply to flush away toxins and rebuild cells. Make water-rich foods (raw vegetables and fresh fruits) an integral part of your daily diet. When you are thirsty, drink pure (distilled or spring) water or fresh fruit or vegetable juice. Avoid swilling colas and other so-called "soft drinks"—they are filled with additives and empty calories.
- **Minimize additional salt and sugar.** A balanced diet will give you plenty of natural salts and sugars. Too much salt can contribute to hypertension and other maladies; excess sugar distorts your metabolism and loads you with useless calories. Avoid being seduced by the short-term energy surge that seems to come from a sugary snack—which is usually soon followed by a depression of vitality. Aim to stop sprinkling salt or spooning sugar onto your foods; at the very least, taste your food before you do so.
- **Moderate your intake of fats, and minimize saturated fats.** Use healthy cold-pressed oils such as canola, olive, and flaxseed; avoid margarine altogether.
- **Enjoy meat, but don't overdo it.** One serving per day is the recommended maximum. When you do eat meat, make sure it is "free range." Avoid eating animals that have been fed growth hormones, antibiotics, and other toxins.
- **Vary your diet.** A varied diet is more likely to be balanced and enjoyable.
- **Drink some caffeine.** Moderate caffeine intake improves short-

term alertness and mental acuity. The odd cup of tea or coffee may be helpful before match play.

- **Drink some alcohol.** According to actuarial statistics, moderate alcohol consumption (defined as no more than two glasses of wine or two beers per day) prolongs the average lifespan by two years. (It goes without saying that drinking beyond moderation has the opposite effect, shortening life and taxing the nervous system.) Despite some World Championship competitors' legendary imbibing, alcohol definitely harms short-term mental acuity and should be avoided for twenty-four hours before match play. Save the champagne for the victory celebration!
- **Don't eat, dine.** "Grabbing a bite" and "eating on the run" lead to a poor diet and much indigestion. Discipline yourself to sit down and enjoy every meal. Create an aesthetically pleasing environment: a nice place setting, flowers, an artful presentation of even the simplest food. Pleasant atmosphere and unhurried pace improve digestion, equanimity, and the quality of life.
- Most important of all, **listen to your body** before every meal and determine what you actually want to eat. If in doubt, imagine how you will feel after eating the food. Then pause for a few moments before eating and bring your awareness to the present moment. Savor the smell, taste, and texture of every bite. And enjoy every meal.

Advice given by the Spanish author Luis Ramirez de Lucena in *Repeticion de Amores y Arte de Axedres* (1497), the earliest printed work on chess, included the following hint: "Try to play soon after your opponent has eaten or drunk freely." This was echoed by the Italian Carrera in *Il Gioco Degli Scacchi* (1617), who gave instructions on how to prepare for a chess game. "Abstain some days from meat to clear the brain, as also to let blood . . . take both purgatives and emetics to drive the humours from the body . . . above all be sure to confess sins and receive spiritual absolution just before play in order to counteract the demoniacal influence of magic spells."

BODY AWARENESS AND POISE

Every martial art emphasizes the importance of stance and posture. Karate and aikido adepts consider the development of *shizentai* ("natural posture") to be an essential key to progress. The "stance" for chess players is sitting at the board. Unnatural at best, prolonged sitting stresses the disks of the lumbar spine and is a major cause of lower-back pain. Pain and discomfort sap energy that should be invested in making the right moves. Most chess competitors are so focused on their board position that they overlook the importance of body position. You can prevent back pain and improve your posture, poise, and concentration by applying the following guidelines:

- Always warm up and stretch before playing.
- Consider bringing your own ergonomically designed chair. (Avoid chairs with deep hollows in the seat or back.)
- Experiment with a rolled-up towel as a neck or lumbar support.
- Keep your feet squarely on the floor, with your knees slightly lower than your hips. (If your feet do not reach the floor, use telephone books or another form of foot rest.)
- Take regular breaks, every fifteen to twenty minutes, to stand and stretch.
- Monitor yourself to prevent contractions and contortions.
- Cultivate poise through a dynamic alignment of your head, neck, and torso.

The most effective way of learning poise is the technique developed in 1896 by F. M. Alexander. Alexander discovered that most of us habitually shorten and stiffen the muscles of the neck, thereby interfering with the balance of the head. The average head weighs ten to fifteen pounds; if it is off balance it causes a pattern of contraction that compresses the spine and throws the whole body out of alignment. Misalignment places undue pressure on internal organs, impedes breathing, and disturbs coordination. Lessons in the Alexander technique guide you to change your thinking so you can outwit this contraction pattern. Appropriate training in the technique requires the assistance of a qualified teacher. (Contact the Society of Teachers of the Alexander Technique; for addresses see page 244.)

Musashi believed that physical attitude and mental posture are inseparable: "You should make your normal stance your fighting stance and your fighting stance your normal stance."

MEDITATION

Meditation has always been part of martial arts training. Regular meditative practice cultivates equanimity and hence better decision-making in the face of attack. In his classic work *The Relaxation Response,* Dr. Herbert Benson reported an in-depth scientific study of the psychological and physiological benefits of various styles of meditation. He found that regular meditation practice can help to lower high blood pressure and to counteract the effects of everyday stress. Other researchers have shown that meditation improves reaction time and clarity of attention. Of course, when you hit the right rhythm, thinking about chess and, indeed, playing it can become a form of meditation.

THE SAMURAI CHESS WARM-UP

We have designed a four-part mind/body warm-up specially for mental athletes. While each part has its own value and can be practiced independently, maximum benefit will be gained by approaching the four parts in sequence.

The warm-up begins with a procedure for cultivating poise drawn from the Alexander Technique. This is followed by some easy stretches and some "ki-development" exercises (*ki* is your personal current of vital power) drawn from the art of aikido. We conclude with a simple "centering" meditation.

The balanced resting state

To benefit from this procedure you simply need a quiet, warm place, some carpeted floor space, and a few paperback books. (For maximum benefit, ask an Alexander teacher to guide you.) For best results, practice the balanced resting state when you wake up, when you come home from work, and before going to bed. The procedure is especially valuable before engaging in competition.

1. Stand with your back to a wall, your buttocks and shoulder blades lightly touching it. Measure the distance from the wall to the back of your head, then add ½ inch to 1 inch. That's how high you should stack the paperback books on the floor. Walk away until your distance from the books equals your height. Stand with your feet shoulder-width apart. Let your hands rest gently at your sides. Facing away from the books, look straight ahead with a soft, alert focus. Pause for a few moments.

2. Become aware of the contact of your feet on the floor, and notice the distance from your feet to the top of your head. Keep your eyes open and alive, and listen to the sounds around you.

3. Maintaining this expansive awareness, kneel lightly and easily so that you are resting on one knee. Then move so that you are sitting on the floor, supporting yourself with your hands behind you, feet in front and flat on the floor, knees bent. Avoid holding your breath.

4. Tilt your head forward just a little to ensure that you are not tightening your neck muscles and pulling your head back. Lie back and gently roll your spine along the floor so that your

head rests on the books. The books should be positioned so that they support your head at the place where your neck ends and your head begins. If your head is not well positioned, pause, reach back with one hand, and support your head while using the other hand to place the books in the proper position. Keep your feet flat on the floor, with your knees pointing up to the ceiling and your hands resting on the floor or loosely folded on your chest. Allow the weight of your body to be fully supported by the floor. Avoid fidgeting or wriggling around to "get comfortable." If you are uncomfortable, start again from the beginning.

5. To reap the benefit of this procedure, rest in this position. As you rest, gravity will lengthen your spine and "undo" unnecessary twists and tensions. Keep your eyes open to avoid dozing. You may wish to bring your attention to the flow of your breathing (without trying to change it) and to the gentle pulsation of your body. Be aware of the ground supporting your back, allowing your shoulders to rest as your back widens. Let your neck be free as your whole body lengthens and expands.

6. After you have rested from five to twenty minutes, get up slowly, being careful to avoid stiffening or shortening your body as you return to a standing position. In order to achieve a smooth transition, decide when you are going to move, and then roll gently onto your front, maintaining your new integration and expansion. Ease your way into a crawling position, and then onto one knee. With your head leading the movement upward, stand.

7. Pause for a few moments . . . listen . . . eyes alive. Again, feel your feet on the floor, and notice the distance between your feet and the top of your head. You may be surprised to discover that the distance has expanded. As you move into your day, think about "not doing" anything that interferes with this expansion, ease and buoyancy.

Stretch for flexibility

Pelvic turns

Stand fully upright with your feet slightly more than shoulder-width apart and your knees slightly bent. Begin by turning your pelvis to the left as far you can without straining your knees. Then turn to the right as far you can without straining your knees, and continue moving from left to right in an easy, relaxed rhythm. Keep your spine perfectly upright and allow your arms to swing freely and gently as you move. After 20 to 30 turns, extend the turn of your pelvis farther, allowing your opposite heel to rise from the ground (i.e., if you are facing left, your right heel will rise). Keep your eyes open and alive and enjoy watching the world whirl by. Allow your arms to swing freely as you perform 20 to 30 repetitions.

Arm circles

Stand fully upright with your feet slightly more than shoulder-width apart and your knees slightly bent. Rotate your arms freely from the shoulder joint so that they circle forward (10 to 15 times) and then backward (10 to 15 times).

Knee, pelvis, and head circles

Standing with your knees together, bend them as far as you can without lifting your heels off the ground. Placing your hands on your kneecaps, make a gentle circling motion with your knees on a plane parallel to the ground. Do this four to six times in each direction. Then, standing upright, feet shoulder-width apart, rotate your pelvis in a wide circling motion on a parallel plane, four to six times in each direction. Next, imagine you have a giant calligraphy brush pointing straight up from the center of your head. Rotate your head as though you were drawing the largest possible Zen circle on the ceiling with your imaginary brush, letting your neck lengthen and relax as you move. Do this four to six times in each direction.

Hamstring release

Sit on the floor with your legs stretched out in front of you, spine upright. Tuck your right foot close-in to your left thigh. Turn toward your left foot, and reach straight up to the ceiling with your hands. Bending from the hip joints and allowing your spine to lengthen as you move, stretch out over your left leg and exhale deeply, reaching out toward your left foot.

Grasp whatever part of your leg you can comfortably reach and think of melting into the stretch. Each time you exhale, allow your hands to ease farther in the direction of your foot. For extra stretch, point the heel of the left foot away from you as you point your toes toward your nose. After 30 seconds, ease back into an upright pose and gently rock your left leg from side to side with both hands. Then do the same stretch to the other side.

Cross-lateral stretch

Lie on your back with your arms spread out to each side. Cross your right leg over your body and let your right knee rest on the floor (see illustration, page 169). Your right shoulder blade will probably come up off the floor. So, keeping your right knee on the ground, think, as you exhale deeply, of allowing your right shoulder blade to ease back toward the ground. (Do *not* force the stretch.) After thirty seconds, switch sides and repeat.

Knee-hugging

Resting flat on your back, bring your knees up toward your chest, so that your lower legs are parallel to the floor. Gently hold your knees there for 30 seconds. Remember to breathe with full exhalation. This stretch is particularly useful in easing lower-back tension.

Ki-development exercises

1. Stand upright with your feet shoulder-width apart. Using your right hand, vigorously pound your left arm from the shoulder down to the fingertips. Imagine that you are chasing all the static, blocked energy out of your arm. Next, pound your right arm the same way. In clockwise rotation, pound your stomach, then your chest in classic Tarzan fashion. Now, with both hands slap your left leg vigorously, starting at the top of your thigh. Imagine chasing stiffness and fatigue down your leg, through your knee, and out through your toes. Do the same thing with your right leg. Now, with both hands, pound your rear end and then, gently, your lower back. Next massage your neck, scalp, forehead, and temples. Mush your cheeks around and massage your jaw.

2. Now, without raising your shoulders, lift your arms up over your head and shake them for about ten seconds so that your whole body vibrates. Maintaining a lively, upright posture, let your hands fall to your sides while breathing out fully with an audible AHHHHH. Repeat this three times, allowing the AHHHHHH to become richer and fuller each time.

3. Next, stand with your left foot forward, at right angles to your right foot, so that if you drew your left foot straight back it would form a T instead of an L. Keep your spine upright and your knees slightly bent. With your feet remaining flat on the floor, transfer your body weight forward so that the base of your spine is in line with your left heel. Then, maintaining a relaxed upright poise (be sure to avoid leaning forward or back with your upper body), shift your weight back so that the base of your spine is over your right big toe. Move forward and back rhythmically. As you shift forward extend your arms like whips straight in front of you. As your weight moves back, let your hands draw into the front of your hips as though you were rowing. Once you have the gist of the movement, add sound: From the depths of your belly say "Aaaaeeehh" as you move forward and "Hohhhh" as you move back. Do this for a minute and then switch feet and repeat. But this time, after saying "Aaaaeeehh" on the way forward, say "saaahhh" on the way back. When you have finished, stand squarely with your feet shoulder-width apart and feel your feet on the ground.

4. Imagine that you are rooted into the center of the Earth. Breathe in through your nose, imagining the *ki* in the air filling your entire being. As you exhale through your mouth, let the breath wash away any remaining static energy. Maintaining your sense of connection with the ground, simultaneously project your awareness up from the point just below your navel. Imagine a stream of pure energy pouring up through your spine and out of the top of your head, connecting you with the heavens. Your body stands as a bridge between heaven and earth. Stretch your arms out to the sides and then up over your head. Then bring your hands together, left over right, at the point just below your navel. Let your mind rest at this point like a lotus blossom floating on a clear pond.

Centering meditation

1. Sit in a comfortable, upright position, in a chair or on the floor in a cross-legged or lotus position. Alternatively, experiment with sitting in *seiza*, the seated posture of the Samurai. However you choose to sit, the important point is to maintain a vertical, lengthening spine.

2. Begin by closing your eyes and scanning your body with your awareness. Gently bring your attention to your feet, ankles, lower legs, knees, thighs, pelvis, lower back, upper back, stomach, chest, shoulders, upper arms, elbows, forearms, wrists, hands, fingers, face, neck, and head. Gently ask each part of your body to relax.

3. Now open your eyes and softly focus them at a point on the floor, a few feet in front of you. Place your left hand over your right (palms up), and with your elbows nestled against your torso let your hands rest, pressing lightly against your lower belly. This area, a few inches below the navel, is called *hara*, the human body's center of gravity. The Samurai believed it to

be the center of the life force. (*Hara-kiri*, the vulgar expression for *seppuku*, means "cutting the vital center.")

4. Now bring your attention to the flow of your breathing. As you inhale through your nose, imagine that you are drawing the life force of the universe into your hara. Exhale through your mouth, slowly and completely, imagining that you are exorcising impurities and anxieties. At first, practice this simple meditation for just a few minutes at a time. When you have finished, focus your eyes on a point across the room, then stand up slowly and carefully.

Now you are lengthened, flexible, energized, centered, and ready to apply the Seven Samurai Principles in your martial arts encounters, competitive chess games, business meetings, and, indeed, any life situation that calls on your maximum mental and physical activation.

PART IV

THE SEVEN SAMURAI PRINCIPLES

SHAPING UP AS A SAMURAI

Part Four explains the seven principles of successful martial combat and how to apply them in chess. Each principle is derived from our extensive study of the martial arts, and represents the essence of the knowledge necessary to win in combat and on the chessboard. Each principle is introduced through the words of legendary masters of chess or the martial arts, and is illustrated by a classic game. The games are by champions whose styles are supreme manifestations of each principle. Finally, a series of chess problems allows you to test your grasp of each principle. These are the Seven Samurai Principles:

- Take the Initiative: Attack
- Follow Through: Go for the Knockout
- Impenetrable Defense: No Openings
- Timing: Control the Tempo
- Distance: Control the Position
- Master Surprise and Deception
- Yield to Win: The Art of Sacrifice

13

TAKE THE INITIATIVE: ATTACK

In his book *Chess Fundamentals* (1921), José Raoul Capablanca, World Chess Champion from 1921 to 1927, wrote:

> Direct and violent attacks must be carried out *en masse* with full force, to ensure their success. The opponent must be overcome at all costs; the attack cannot be broken off, since in all such cases that means defeat.

Morihei Ueshiba was an enlightened genius who saw beyond the win/lose paradigm to the essential oneness of humanity. His philosophy "true *budo* is love" led him to emphasize "protecting the opponent," a win/win approach to resolving conflict without violence. Of all the martial arts, aikido is perhaps the most evolved, inspiring, and difficult to master. Yet Ueshiba's emphasis on harmony and love is frequently misinterpreted. Many people, including would-be aikido practitioners, view the art as a defensive, passive approach to martial encounter. During his lifetime, Ueshiba attracted an ever-growing number of followers, including many of Japan's leading practitioners of judo, ju-jitsu, karate, and kendo. These formidable and arrogant warriors became receptive to the founder's sophisticated philosophies after he had wiped the floor with them! From the film of Ueshiba in action, which we have studied carefully, it is clear that in every encounter he takes the initiative.

On a considerably less exalted level, the average palooka in the boxing gym lives by one simple maxim: "Hit them before they hit you."

Be the firstest with the mostest.

—U.S. General Nathan Bedford Forrest,
said to have killed no fewer than 31 people in duels

In chess, White always plays first, and therefore starts with a small advantage. But frequently the first player to mount a coordinated assault gains the ultimate advantage. A strong attack sets the opponent "back on his heels," upsets his timing and rhythm, and puts you in control.

It is a correct maxim that the best defense is a good offense.

—Bruce Lee, *Tao of Jeet Kune Do*

PAUL MORPHY—THE IMPERATOR OF INITIATIVE

Paul Morphy is our choice for supreme exemplar of the first Samurai principle: "take the initiative: attack." An American lawyer born in 1837, Morphy is often regarded as the greatest chess genius the world has ever seen. He established his reputation as a prodigy in New Orleans at the age of 12, when he beat the Hungarian master Johann Lowenthal. He dominated the field in the first American Chess Congress in New York in 1857, defeating the German master Louis Paulsen in the final. There followed a triumphal tour of London and Paris in which Morphy scattered the masters of European chess like so much chaff before the wind. As a diversion he entertained spectators with his virtuosity at blindfold chess, taking on eight opponents simultaneously without seeing any of the boards.

Morphy's victims in a series of individual challenge matches included Lowenthal, Harrwitz, and Anderssen. His superiority was outstanding, and his only disappointment was his failure to arrange a match against Howard Staunton, still the world's most famous player, if no longer the strongest. Had there been an official World Championship in those days, Morphy would undoubtedly have won it.

Returning home in 1859, Morphy was given a hero's welcome. Chess mania gripped America, and new clubs, tournaments, and books flowered. Yet, in a curious and eerie premonition of Bobby Fischer's long withdrawal from public competition after his World Championship in 1972, Paul Morphy suddenly retired from serious combat. After his European tour he never played first-class opponents again, confining himself to simultaneous displays or casual games with amateurs, to whom he gave heavy odds.

White: Louis Paulsen; Black: Paul Morphy
New York 1857
Four Knights Game

This game was played in the final of the first American Chess Congress, in which Paul Morphy defeated his opponent Louis Paulsen. It illustrates with crystal clarity the overwhelming impact of Morphy's exuberantly attacking style.

1	e4	e5
2	♘f3	♘c6
3	♘c3	♘f6
4	♗b5	♗c5
5	0-0	0-0
6	♘xe5	

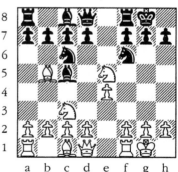

White's capture on move six introduces a simple exchanging combination known as the "fork trick." The point is that the reply ♘xe5 allows 7 d4, attacking two black pieces at once. But:

6	. . .	♖e8
7	♘xc6	dxc6
8	♗c4	

Morphy, the genius of attack, does not now fall for the invitation to reply 8 . . . ♘xe4. This would have allowed 9 ♘xe4 ♖xe4 10 ♗xf7+ ♔xf7 11 ♕f3+ with a double attack on Black's king and rook. Instead he continues:

8	. . .	b5
9	♗e2	♘xe4
10	♘xe4	♖xe4
11	♗f3	♖e6
12	c3	

Black is given the chance to take the initiative and Morphy is quick to exploit this mistake by powerfully seizing control of the resulting hole in White's fortress. Paulsen should have played 12 d3.

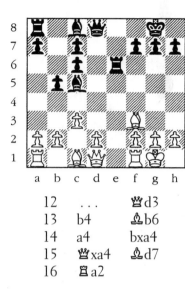

12	. . .	♕d3
13	b4	♗b6
14	a4	bxa4
15	♕xa4	♗d7
16	♖a2	

It is still not too late for White to play 16 ♕a6 to challenge the black queen. But:

| 16 | . . . | ♖ae8 |
| 17 | ♕a6 | ♕xf3! |

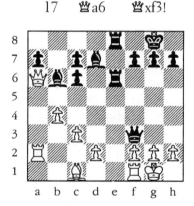

This splendid queen sacrifice must have come as a terrible shock to Paulsen. Black gets just a bishop for his queen, but the important thing is that the g-file is wrenched open, so that Black's rook can join in the onslaught.

18	gxf3	♖g6+
19	♔h1	♗h3
20	♖d1	♗g2+
21	♔g1	♗xf3+
22	♔f1	♗g2+
23	♔g1	♗h3+
24	♔h1	♗xf2

Note the awesome power of Black's pieces, which are working in unison.

White is now utterly helpless and must give back the queen to stave off checkmate for a further few moves.

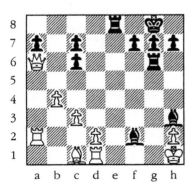

25	♕f1	♗xf1
26	♖xf1	♖e2
27	♖a1	♖h6
28	d4	♗e3

Here Paulsen resigned. Had he not done so, there would have followed:

29	♗xe3	♖hxh2+
30	♔g1	♖eg2
	checkmate	

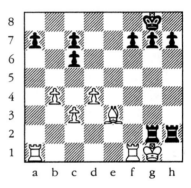

A fantastic example of the devastating force exerted by Black's rooks, doubled and rampaging along White's second rank.

14

FOLLOW THROUGH:
GO FOR THE KNOCKOUT

Everything can collapse. Houses, bodies, and enemies collapse when their rhythm becomes deranged.

In large-scale strategy, when the enemy starts to collapse you must pursue him without letting the chance go. If you fail to take advantage of your enemies' collapse, they may recover.

In single combat, the enemy sometimes loses timing and collapses. If you let this opportunity pass, he may recover and not be so negligent thereafter. Fix your eye on the enemy's collapse, and chase him, attacking so that you do not let him recover. You must do this. The chasing attack is with a strong spirit. You must utterly cut the enemy down so that he does not recover his position.

– *Musashi*

In Hollywood movies the "good guy"often fells his opponent in a fight with a brilliant combination of punches, only to turn his back while his attacker recovers and whacks him in the head from behind with a chair. In real combat we train to finish the opponent by knocking him out cold. The best fighters from western boxing and competitive bu-jitsu all hone this "killer instinct." In real life, mercy and compassion are highly admirable and desirable qualities, but during a chess game they are irrelevant. (After you have vanquished your opponent is the moment to offer encouraging words and a beverage.)

ZANSHIN

When your attacking strategy yields an advantage, you must stay focused and capitalize on it. Even if you have captured material early, do not let up. Big-game hunters in Africa say, "It is the dead lion that gets up and eats you." The Samurai aphorism "After the battle, tighten your helmet straps," is a reminder that you should not let your guard down just because you have won—apparently. In modern Japanese martial arts, this quality is called zanshin— "continuing mind."

There is good reason to "tighten your helmet straps," despite an overwhelming advantage. You can always be suckered into a draw through stalemate, or you can lose outright through wickedly clever play from an opponent who appears to have nothing to lose. The following two examples—the sucker stalemate and the dramatic victory when all seems lost—show how a "dead lion" can still get up and eat a player who has lost zanshin.

White: Larry Evans; Black: Sammy Reshevsky
U.S. Championship 1964

Black to move

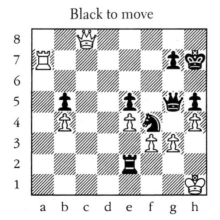

In this needle game from the U.S. Championship between two top American Grandmasters, Black is a knight ahead and would win easily with virtually any move. He could even play 1 . . . ♕g6 since White dare not capture the knight.

Instead, Reshevsky fell for the sucker punch by playing 1 . . . ♕xg3. Now White had his chance, and rose from the dead with the stunning 2 ♕g8+ ♔xg8 3 ♖xg7+.

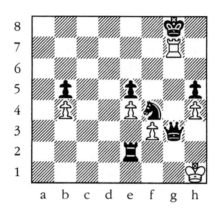

White's amazing series of sacrifices forces a draw. From the diagram 3 . . . ♕xg7 is stalemate as is 3 . . . ♔xg7. Alternatively, if the black king tries to run away from the checks with 3 . . . ♔h8, then 4 ♖h7+ ♔g8 5 ♖g7+ ♔f8 6 ♖f7+ ♔e8 7 ♖e7+, and so on *ad infinitum.* The white rook pursues the black king like a rottweiler, yapping and snapping at his heels. Whenever the rook is taken, the stalemate draw becomes automatic. This is perhaps the most dramatic example in top-flight tournament chess of this drawing theme.

The second example features the normally imperturbable and virtually undefeatable Petrosian. This was the second-biggest blunder of his career. (See page 153 for the worst.)

White: Petrosian; Black: Gligoric
Belgrade 1956

In the diagram position, White can win easily with 1 ♖xe8+ ♛xe8 2 ♗h6 (threatening mate on g7) 2 . . . ♞f3+ 3 ♔g2 ♛e5 when 4 ♖a8 strikes Black down from a new direction.

White to play

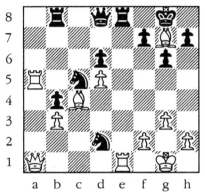

Instead Petrosian reversed the order of his moves. He played 1 ♗h6, which was immediately crushed by 1 . . . ♖xe1+ 2 ♛xe1 ♞f3+

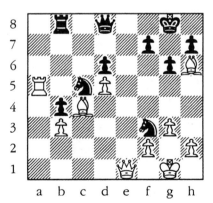

Now the black knight has forked the white king and queen, so White resigned.

The ultimate model for the second Samurai chess principle is Adolf Anderssen, a German Grandmaster who won the first ever international tournament, staged in London in 1851, and remained a dominating figures in world chess for two decades. Anderssen was noted for the brutality and elegance of his finishing power.

White: Adolf Anderssen; Black: Lionel Kieseritsky
London 1851
King's Gambit

This game was played during the 1851 Great Exhibition. The vanquished Lionel Kieseritsky, chess tutor at the Café de la Regence, Paris, where he gave lessons at 5 francs an hour, was so impressed by the brilliance of Anderssen's play that he immediately telegraphed the moves to a waiting audience in Paris. Ever since, this game has been known by the unimprovable sobriquet the Immortal Game.

1	e4	e5
2	f4	exf4
3	♗c4	♕h4+
4	♔f1	b5

Here Black sacrifices his pawn to lure White's bishop away from its attacking position and to create an avenue of development for his own queen's bishop from b7. In 1851 even masters regarded this as sufficient compensation for the loss of a pawn.

5	♗xb5	♘f6
6	♘f3	♕h6
7	d3	♘h5

This is a mistake. Black would have been better advised to play . . . ♗b7. The knight's transparent threat of . . . ♘g3+ is too easily parried.

8	♘h4	♕g5
9	♘f5	c6
10	g4	♘f6

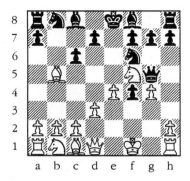

Black here evidently expects to win White's g4 pawn, anticipating the continuation 11 ♗c4 ♛xg4. Instead of obliging in this fashion, White gives up his bishop—the first of many sacrifices in this brilliant game. Anderssen demonstrates superb risk assessment in this game. If his attack does not break through, he will certainly lose because of his heavy material sacrifices.

| 11 | ♖g1 | cxb5 |
| 12 | h4 | ♛g6 |

White has the initiative—every move of White's now poses a forced threat.

| 13 | h5 | ♛g5 |
| 14 | ♛f3 | |

White now poses the terrible new threat of ♗xf4, trapping Black's queen. In order to create an avenue of escape, Black has to retreat one of the few pieces he has developed.

14	...	♞g8
15	♗xf4	♛f6
16	♞c3	♗c5
17	♞d5	

This heralds the introduction to a grandiose combination in which White sacrifices both rooks and his queen to deliver checkmate.

| 17 | ... | ♛xb2 |
| 18 | ♗d6 | ♛xa1+ |

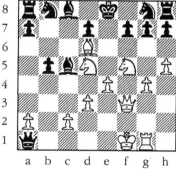

Black wins his first rook.

| 19 | ♔e2 | ♗xg1 |

Black does not believe White's attack and takes the second rook. White is now the colossal total of two rooks and a bishop down. He must go remorselessly for the most accurate knockout blow; otherwise Black will recover and inevitably win on sheer material.

| 20 | e5 | ♘a6 |
| 21 | ♘xg7+ | ♚d8 |

Now, to cap all White's earlier efforts, comes the queen sacrifice.

| 22 | ♕f6+ | ♘xf6 |
| 23 | ♗e7 | check-mate |

The most spectacular knockout in the entire history of chess:

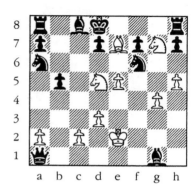

It's like a game of chess: you synchronize the action of your pieces, then BLAM.

—Line from *Independence Day*, the top-grossing movie blockbuster of 1996

15

IMPENETRABLE DEFENSE: NO OPENINGS

In *Aikido and the Harmony of Nature*, Mitsugi Saotome relates the following story of impenetrable defense: no openings.

Once in Ayabe, O Sensei [the reverential Japanese title for Ueshiba] . . . was visited by a very accomplished kendo master. Anxious to test himself and to prove a point, the kendo master challenged O Sensei. They walked into the garden together, the kendo master carrying his *katana*, O Sensei empty handed. The sun flashed off the brightly polished steel as the kendo master moved into his *kamae* [attack stance], O Sensei standing quietly before him. And they stood. Sweat began to break on the kendo master's forehead, rolling down his cheeks like tears. It fell like a thousand prisms from the strained and glistening muscles of his powerfully developed forearms. And still they stood. O Sensei calm and detached, aware but not waiting, only reflected the image of the man and the sun-drenched steel before him. Five, seven, maybe ten minutes passed. Exhausted from the struggle of attempting to attack the universe, the kendo man surrendered. He had been unable to move.

The greatest pleasure of boxing is making the other guy miss.

—Floyd Patterson, who in 1956 became the youngest man
to win the world heavyweight championship

Of course, even after completing *Samurai Chess*, we do not expect that you will be able to stop your opponent moving the pieces through the sheer power of your presence alone. We do aim to offer you the keys to sound defensive play. Just as the best defense is a good offense, a solid defense provides the underpinning of every successful attack.

Like a great martial artist, [Karpov] had the bewildering ability to deflect the power of lethal blows back upon his opponent. He was a defensive genius, who often won by absorbing his opponent's power, as Kasparov said, like a spider. For decades over the board, he had defended the indefensible, wriggling out of mortal predicaments to come out on top. He had done this, in part, through an ability to appear cool and confident even while under heavy attack. Kasparov had said that Karpov was difficult to hit. How can you hit an opponent if you cannot find him?

—American chess writer Fred Waitzkin on Anatoly Karpov

Aron Nimzowitsch—The Boffin of Blockade

The Grandmaster who best illustrates the third Samurai principle is Aron Nimzowitsch. He was a dominant figure among the post–World War I generation of hypermodern Grandmasters whose cast of chess thought was impregnated with the twisted logic of years of carnage on European battlefields. Their play was enigmatic, even discordant by classical standards, but their creations radiated the same strange beauty as the work of Picasso, Kafka, Duchamp, and Stravinsky in other realms.

White: Sämisch; Black: Nimzowitsch
Copenhagen 1923
Queen's Indian Defense

In this game Nimzowitsch interprets the military techniques prevalent in World War I in a chessboard paradigm. Trench campaigns, blockade, and defense in depth are all organized first to blunt White's attacking potential and then to drain the enemy position of all energy, prior to the final strike.

1	d4	♘f6
2	c4	e6
3	♘f3	b6
4	g3	♗b7
5	♗g2	♗e7
6	♘c3	0-0
7	0-0	d5
8	♘e5	c6
9	cxd5	

9 e4 places Black under considerably more pressure.

9	. . .	cxd5
10	♗f4	a6
11	♖c1	b5

Nimzowitsch steals some space on the queen's flank. The correct reaction by White would have been the brisk counterattack 12 a4.

12	♕b3

Sämisch misses his chance. The text move looks plausible; indeed it is hard to believe, given the apparently fluid nature of White's development and the virtually symmetrical pawn structure, that White's position will be reduced to rubble in a mere 13 moves.

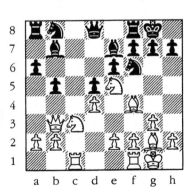

12	...	♞c6
13	♞xc6	♝xc6
14	h3	♛d7
15	♚h2	

Sämisch is running out of ideas, and from this point on Nimzowitsch gradually assumes the initiative.

15	...	♞h5
16	♝d2	f5
17	♛d1	b4

Inexorably, White's pieces are driven backward and Black's strategy of suffocation takes grip.

18	♞b1	♝b5
19	♜g1	♝d6
20	e4	

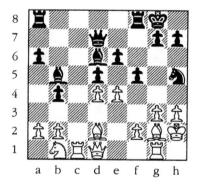

A cunning move that would have floored many op-

ponents. At a stroke, Black's loose knight on h5 is attacked by White's queen, and if Black defends the knight with 20...g6, then 21 exd5 throws Black's camp into turmoil. Nevertheless, Nimzowitsch has organized his defenses in depth and is ready for this.

20	...	fxe4

The perfect response. Nimzowitsch sacrifices his knight for two pawns and simultaneously enters the breach in White's forces, the traditionally vulnerable pawn on f2. The conclusion is spectacular.

21	♛xh5	♜xf2

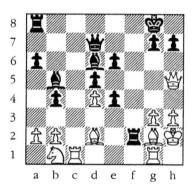

22	♛g5	♜af8
23	♚h1	♜8f5

24	♛e3	♝d3
25	♖ce1	h6

White resigns

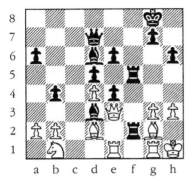

This is one of the most amazing finishes in the entire history of chess. On a crowded board, White has succumbed to the Zugzwang syndrome. Zugzwang, a German chess term imported into English, means "compulsion to move." White has been totally block-

aded, and any move he makes leads to disaster. Normally Zugzwang occurs only in the endgame with few pieces on the board. To have achieved this at the height of a middle-game struggle almost defies belief.

Let us see what happens if White tries to make a move:

a) 26 ♖d1 or 26 ♖c1, then 26 . . . ♖e2 traps the white queen.
b) If White moves his king with 26 ♔h2, then 26 . . . ♖5f3 also traps the queen since White's bishop on g2 is now pinned.
c) 26 g4 ♖5f3 27 ♝xf3 ♖h2 checkmate.
d) If 26 ♝c1, then 26 . . . ♝xb1 wins material, or if 26 ♝f1, then 26 . . . ♝xf1 does the same.

Concealed beneath the stifling blockade of the greatest defensive geniuses lurks a devastating ability to counterpunch.

16

TIMING: CONTROL THE TEMPO

Yamaoku Tesshu emphasized that the essence of combat was timing.

> Natural victory is to strike at precisely the right moment. When a hawk catches its prey, it does so at the perfect instant. Swordsmanship is the same. Move at the right moment and there is true victory, one hundred out of one hundred times; fail to do so, and all will be lost.

> Joe Louis, the great boxing champion, said that he knew that his timing had gone and it was time to "hang up his gloves" when he could see his opponents' openings. In his prime, Louis commented, he didn't "see" the openings, he just entered them and knocked his opponent out.

Musashi also understood that timing was the essence of strategy: "There is timing in everything. . . . You win in battles by knowing the enemy's timing and thus using a timing which the enemy does not expect."

Timing embraces the management of the clock and also the rhythm of the game. You must learn to dictate the tempo, to disturb your opponent's rhythm and to make him waste valuable time.

That little fragment of time (one beat in a cadence) which is the most suitable to accomplish effective action is called "tempo."

An excellent moment to launch an attack is when the opponent is preparing an attack.

—Bruce Lee, *Tao of Jeet Kune Do*

WILHELM STEINITZ—THE TIGER OF THE TEMPO

The Austrian player Wilhelm Steinitz was the first official World Chess Champion, from 1886 to 1894, and possibly the game's most profound thinker. His deep insights into defensive play and into the accumulation of small but enduring advantages changed the outlook of an entire generation of Grandmasters and baffled his opponents for many years. Before Steinitz, everybody believed that winning depended on both inventiveness and luck, and that rapid kingside attacks were always the most effective strategy. After Steinitz, everyone saw that no attack could succeed unless it was launched at the proper time with a prior clear strategic advantage. It was understood that even relatively minor advantages—doubled, isolated or backward pawns, a queenside pawn majority, or two bishops versus bishop and knight—were often highly significant, and that the best form of defense was to avoid permanent positional weaknesses. Paul Morphy had shown the way in open positions; Steinitz illuminated the paths in the infinitely more subtle closed positions. Some experts have claimed that his defensive barricades were the chessboard precursors of the trench warfare tactics of World War I.

In bringing about this major transformation Steinitz suffered much abuse, but he displayed enormous confidence and participated in controversy with obstinate and even bitter relish. Born in Prague in 1836, Steinitz moved to Vienna in 1858 and then to London eight years later, where he dominated British chess and wrote for *Field*. In 1882 he moved to New York, where he founded and edited *International Chess* magazine.

White: Wilhelm Steinitz; Black: Mikhail Tchigorin
Havana 1892
Ruy Lopez

This was the fourth game in an official World Championship match played between Steinitz, the reigning champion, and Mikhail Tchigorin, his persistent Russian challenger. The game was notable for the bracing refreshments the masters consumed during play. Tchigorin was supplied with free brandy, Steinitz with champagne—on doctor's orders, he explained afterward, so as to fortify his nerves. The opening is a version of the Ruy Lopez.

1	e4	e5
2	♘f3	♘c6
3	♗b5	♘f6
4	d3	

The fashionable move nowadays is 4 0-0, but there is

nothing wrong with this quiet reinforcement of the center, and 4 ♕e2 (as suggested by Ruy Lopez himself) is also playable.

4	...	d6
5	c3	g6
6	♘d2	♗g7
7	♘f1	0-0
8	♗a4	♘d7
9	♘e3	♘c5
10	♗c2	♘e6

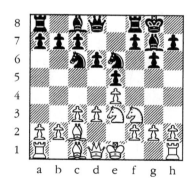

Steinitz now chooses precisely the right moment to start his attack. Black has already committed his king. White can still choose to castle queenside. This is, therefore, the correct time to advance. In contrast, 11 0-0 would be stereotyped and feeble and Black would soon start his own attack based on . . . f5.

11	h4	♘e7
12	h5	d5
13	hxg6	fxg6

Had Black played 13 . . . hxg6 White would still have had no overwhelming advantage. Instead:

14	exd5	♘xd5
15	♘xd5	♕xd5
16	♗b3	♕c6

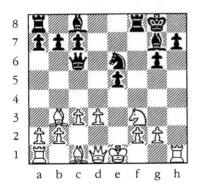

White now controls two powerful open lines toward the black king: the bishop on b3 exerting pressure along the diagonal from c4 to g8 where the black king is, and the rook on h1 attacking in the rook's file toward the defensive black pawn on h7. Given Tchigorin's lack of counterplay, it only remains for Steinitz to mobilize the rest of his forces before the decisive attack inevitably materializes.

17	♕e2	♗d7
18	♗e3	♔h8
19	0-0-0	♖ae8
20	♕f1	

White's fine move opens new avenues of attack.

| 20 | . . . | a5 |

The wretched situation of Black's king leaves him curiously helpless against the coming onslaught. But first White makes a feint in the center, masking his true intentions.

21	d4	exd4
22	♘xd4	♗xd4
23	♖xd4	

There are so many threats at this point (even the simple ♖h4 would be deadly) that Black's knight might as well accept the offer of the rook.

23   ...   ♗xd4
24   ♖xh7+

Sacrifices like these are spectacular, but desperately dangerous for less accomplished players to risk making. In your own games, remember that extra material usually triumphs, so sacrifice like this only if you are sure it works!

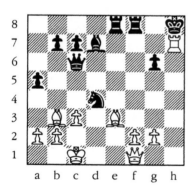

24   ...   ♔xh7
25   ♕h1+

Just as everyone was waiting for execution along the twin diagonals, Steinitz reveals his true plans with a stunning surprise on a totally different front.

25   ...   ♔g7
26   ♗h6+   ♔f6
27   ♕h4+

Black's king is swiftly chased to its doom.

27   ...   ♔e5
28   ♕xd4+   ♔f5
29   ♕f4   check-
              mate

One of the all-time great victories, with the black king cut down in midboard.

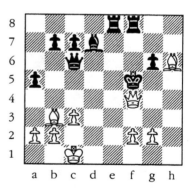

In large-scale strategy, when we see that the enemy has few men, or if he has many men but his spirit is weak and disordered, we knock the hat over his eyes, crushing him utterly. If we crush lightly, he may recover. You must learn the spirit of crushing as if with a hand-grip. In single combat, if the enemy is less skillful than ourself, if his rhythm is disorganized, or if he has fallen into evasive or retreating attitudes, we must crush him straightaway, with no concern for his presence and without allowing him space for breath. It is essential to crush him all at once. The primary thing is not to let him recover his position even a little. You must research this deeply.

— Musashi

17

DISTANCE:
CONTROL THE POSITION

Richard Réti, Grandmaster and inventor of revolutionary chess openings during the 1920s, argued in his book *Masters of the Chess Board* (1933) that

> the real criterion by which to appraise positions is the possibility of breaking through. In general, the player who can move freely over a greater area will place his pieces more advantageously, for a possible breakthrough, than an opponent who is restricted in his movements.

One of the great scenes in the movie *Braveheart* depicts the heavily armed English cavalry charging the bedraggled line of Scottish rebels, led by William Wallace (Mel Gibson). Standing at the front of his troops, Wallace exhorts his men, "Hold . . . Hold . . . Hold . . . " as the cavalry bear down, moments away from trampling them into oblivion. As the ironclad horsemen reach a distance of twelve feet, Wallace screams "Now!" His front line dives backward releasing a row of 10-foot spears upon which the cavalry is impaled instantly. In combat, proper timing goes together with awareness of space and position.

In the Samurai tradition, this awareness is expressed in a simple phrase, *Kami shitoe*, which refers to the thickness of a single sheet of fine rice paper. On one side of the paper is written the *kanji* (character or symbol) of life, on the other the *kanji* of death. To the Samurai, *Kami shitoe* signifies that the difference between life and death is an infinitesimal alteration of position. The art of maintaining the right position and distance relative to the opponent is called *maai* ("the joining of space — harmonious distance"). Skilled martial artists know that the enemy's most powerful strike is harmless if one remains just outside its range. They know that their own best techniques can be executed effectively only from the appropriate position. And they know that positional effectiveness begins and ends with domination of the opponent's center. The same is true in chess.

The maintenance of proper fighting distance has a decisive effect on the outcome of the fight. Acquire the habit!

—Bruce Lee, *Tao of Jeet Kune Do*

In an instant enter the tiniest space.

—Tesshu

José Raoul Capablanca—the supremo of space

The Cuban José Raoul Capablanca was the first modern chess player to become a superstar. When he lost a game to Richard Réti in New York in 1924 it made headlines around the world. He had been considered invincible, a magician of the chessboard, and had not been defeated for more than eight years.

Capablanca, who was born in Havana in 1888, held the World Championship from 1921 to 1927. The story goes that he picked up the moves of chess at the age of four from watching his father play with friends. At twelve he beat Juan Corzo, the Cuban champion. His reputation began to grow when he annihilated Frank Marshall, America's leading Grandmaster, in 1909. Solely because of this win against one of the world's top players, he was invited to a Grandmaster tournament at San Sebastian in 1911. All the contestants were supposed to have won first prize in at least one Grandmaster tournament, and two of the contestants, Aron Nimzowitsch and Ossip Bernstein, both established members of the "Grandmaster Club," protested at the young Cuban's inclusion. The legendary status rapidly engulfing Capablanca required that he should destroy both his detractors at the board, and then that he should win first prize. He accomplished both these feats with ease.

In 1913 Capablanca obtained a position with the Cuban Foreign Office that opened unlimited possibilities for foreign travel and hence for chess. Eight years later the Capablanca legend was crowned when, in his home city, he beat Emanuel Lasker and became the only man in the history of chess not to lose a single game in winning the World Championship.

White: Ossip Bernstein; Black: José Raoul Capablanca
Moscow 1914
Queen's Gambit Declined

Bernstein lost to the young Capablanca in the elite tournament in San Sebastian in 1911, and lost again three years later in the game described here, which elegantly displays Capablanca's genius. Black's crushing 29th move was a thunderbolt.

The standard technique of the Cuban genius was to cast a gradual, virtually imperceptible, but overwhelmingly enmeshing net around the unsuspecting opponent. His thunderbolt in this game is based on a combination of tactical and spatial factors that most seasoned observers would consider to be truly miraculous.

1	d4	d5
2	c4	e6
3	♘f3	♘f6
4	♘c3	♗e7
5	♗g5	0-0
6	e3	♘bd7
7	♖c1	b6
8	cxd5	exd5

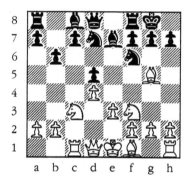

Capablanca was happy to play the Queen's Gambit with either White or Black.

9	♕a4	♗b7
10	♗a6	♗xa6
11	♕xa6	c5

Black risks advancing in the center, even though exchanges may enable White's rook to take up central squares and attack Black's forces.

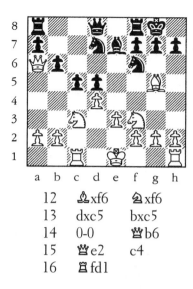

12	♗xf6	♘xf6
13	dxc5	bxc5
14	0-0	♕b6
15	♕e2	c4
16	♖fd1	

White's plan is to bombard Black's two pawns on the c- and d-files. An irony of this game is that Bernstein's eventual success in winning one of these pawns is what actually brings about his downfall.

| 16 | ... | ♖fd8 |
| 17 | ♘d4 | ♗b4 |

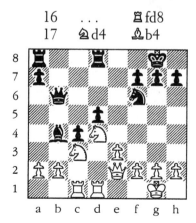

A subtle move. Capablanca prepares to trade his bishop for the white knight, which potentially threatens the black center pawn on d5.

White now launches an energetic diversionary tactic, pressing against the advanced black pawn on c4.

18	b3	♖ac8
19	bxc4	dxc4
20	♖c2	♗xc3
21	♖xc3	♘d5
22	♖c2	c3

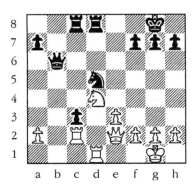

A passed pawn. Is it strong or weak?

Life or death? *Kami shitoe.*

23	♖dc1	♖c5

Now, at long last, White sets in motion a maneuver that wins the bold black pawn which has advanced so far into his camp.

24	♘b3	♖c6
25	♘d4	♖c7
26	♘b5	♖c5

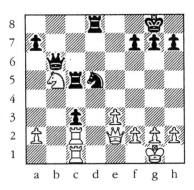

Has Black been outplayed? White has invested a lot of energy in winning Black's pawn, and now he rounds it up. Was this the right thing to do?

27	♘xc3	♘xc3
28	♖xc3	♖xc3
29	♖xc3	

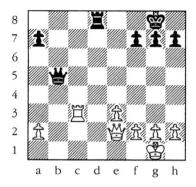

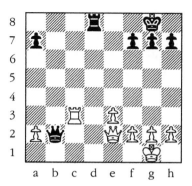

At last, winning the pawn. It appears that White has calculated well, for 29 ... ♛b1+ 30 ♕f1 ♜d1 will lead to 31 ♜c8 checkmate. This is clearly what Bernstein was expecting, but Black played:

29   ...   ♛b2!!

"When the enemy comes running to strike you, step aside, avoid him. Immediately attack and cut him down. . . ."

One of the most famous finishes in chess history—a superb exploitation of space, distance, and the awesome geometry of the chessboard!

Faced with this thunderbolt, White has no choice but to resign. The winning variations now open to Capablanca, all calculated with mathematical precision, are fascinating:

1) 30 ♕xb2 ♜d1 checkmate
2) 30 ♜c8 ♛a1+ 31 ♕f1 ♛xf1+ 32 ♔xf1 ♜xc8 and from here, Black will have no trouble winning with his extra rook.
3) 30 ♜c2 ♛b1+ 31 ♕f1 ♛xc2 again gives Black the advantage of an extra rook.
4) 30 ♕e1 ♛xc3 31 ♕xc3 ♜d1+ 32 ♕e1 ♜xe1 checkmate.

Note the vital significance in all these variations of the leitmotif of the back rank checkmate by queen or rook.

In this game, we have also seen Bernstein becoming obsessed with the local (winning Black's pawn on c3) rather than the global, that is, with the possibility of being checkmated. Musashi has counsel for such situations.

"Rat's head and ox's neck" means that, when we are fighting with the enemy and both he and we have become occupied with small points in an entangled spirit, we must always think of the Way of strategy as being both a rat's head and an ox's neck. Whenever we have become preoccupied with small details, we must suddenly change into a large spirit, interchanging large with small.

This is one of the essences of strategy. It is necessary that the warrior think in this spirit in everyday life. You must not depart from this spirit in large-scale strategy nor in single combat.

18

MASTER SURPRISE AND DECEPTION

Attack by deception, especially, is the attack of the master. We must surprise our opponent and catch the moment of his helplessness.

—Bruce Lee, *Tao of Jeet Kune Do*

In *The Art of War*, Sun Tzu, the Chinese military theorist, wrote:

> All warfare is based on deception. Hence, when able to attack, we must seem unable; when using our forces, we must seem inactive; when we are near, we must make the enemy believe we are far away; when far away, we must make him believe we are near. Hold out bait to entice the enemy. Feign disorder, and crush him. If he is secure at all points, be prepared for him. If he is superior in strength, evade him. If your opponent is of choleric temper, seek to irritate him. Pretend to be weak, that he may grow arrogant. If he is taking his ease, give him no rest. If his forces are united, separate them. Attack him where he is unprepared, appear where you are not expected.

In the art of kendo one strategy of deception is called *suigetsu no heiho*, "the moon in water." In *suigetsu* you "fake" an opening and then surprise your enemy by cutting at the moment he attacks. Faking, feinting, and deception are vital elements in your armory.

BORIS SPASSKY—THE DEMON OF DECEPTION

Boris Vasilievich Spassky is one of the greatest chess players who ever lived. After a volcanic early career, in which he gave full rein to his aggressive genius, he won the World Championship from his Soviet compatriot Tigran Petrosian in 1969. It was a victory to gladden the hearts of the romantics, for, while Petrosian's style had relied on slippery defensive skills and patient consolidation, Spassky was wholeheartedly committed to attack. It seemed that he could look forward to a great and glorious future. But, alas, it was not to be. The first challenge to his reign came from the disconcerting, eccentric American Bobby Fischer. Their match at Reykjavik in 1972 was subjected to a glare of publicity previously unknown in chess, with political and symbolic overtones that overshadowed the purely sporting aspects of the game.

The battering Spassky received in that match knocked the guts out of him. He never succeeded in staging a world title comeback, and in the USSR his reputation was rapidly eclipsed by that of Anatoly Karpov. The restrictions of Soviet life began to irk his free spirit. Within a few years he emigrated to France, the country he now represents at the chess Olympics. But he has never recovered the élan that Fischer's onslaught quenched.

Yet it is for his early buccaneering, before the trauma of Reykjavik, that Boris Spassky deserves to be remembered. His glittering and elegant play produced some of the most excitingly aggressive and deeply surprising attacking games of chess ever executed.

White: Bent Larsen; Black: Boris Spassky
Belgrade 1970
Larsen's Opening

This is a game from the so-called Match of the Century, when the USSR team, led by Spassky, took on the Rest of the World in the Belgrade Trades Union Hall.

Bent Larsen was one of the first modern western Grandmasters to present a serious threat to the Soviet domination of chess. However, he could do little to thwart Spassky, who was at the height of his powers, or to prevent the world team from sliding to eventual defeat.

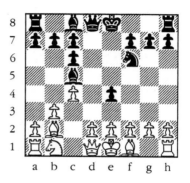

1	b3	e5
2	♗b2	♞c6
3	c4	♞f6
4	♞f3	

This is a risky and provocative move. A safer move would have been 4 e3.

4	...	e4
5	♞d4	♗c5
6	♞xc6	dxc6

For the sake of speedy development, Black (Spassky) has sacrificed his pawn structure, capturing away from the center and weakening his position with doubled pawns on the c-file.

7	e3	♗f5
8	♕c2	♕e7
9	♗e2	0-0-0
10	f4	♞g4

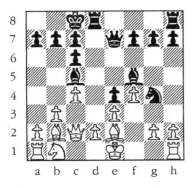

Apparently Black wants to play ... ♕h4+, but this knight move is a feint, with a much more profound purpose.

11	g3	h5
12	h3	h4!

This was a great move, sacrificing a piece in order to blast away the pawn protection around White's king. But the superstar move was yet to come.

13	hxg4	hxg3
14	♖g1	

White is a piece up. How can Black penetrate his defenses?

The passed pawn on g3 is now obviously worth far more than its formal value of one point. It is about to play a key role in the coming attack.

However, White threatens to capture it (♖xg3) and also to take Black's bishop on f5.

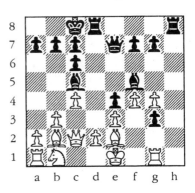

14	...	♖h1!!

This rook swoop is one of the most amazing, surprising, and fantastic moves I have ever seen played. White must capture the rook, but then Black gains vital time to access the h4 square with his queen, with check. White's resistance is annihilated.

15	♖xh1	g2

This is the vital tempo Black has gained, since White's rook is now threatened by capture, with check. White now faces an impossible dilemma. If he preserves the extra rook with 16 ♖g1, then Black will win with 16 ...

♛h4+ 17 ♚d1 ♛h1 18
♜xh1 gxh1(♛)+ 19 ♗f1
♛xf1 checkmate.

What actually happened
was:

16	♜f1	♛h4+
17	♚d1	gxf1(♛)+

White resigned

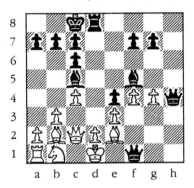

Had he not done so, the
game would have finished
like this:

18	♗xf1	♗xg4+
19	♗e2	♛h1
	checkmate	

Alternatively:

18	♗xf1	♗xg4+
19	♚c1	♛e1+
20	♛d1	♛xd1
	checkmate	

19

YIELD TO WIN:
THE ART OF SACRIFICE

"The glowing power of the sacrifice is irresistible: enthusiasm for sacrifice lies in human nature." So wrote the Austrian Grandmaster Rudolf Spielmann (1883–1942) in his book *The Art of Sacrifice in Chess*.

In normal judo competition one aims to unbalance the opponent and throw him. However, there are times when an opponent is too strong and well balanced to be dispatched by normal methods. This is the time for a drastic measure, the most dramatic of all judo moves, *sutemi-nage*, the sacrifice throw (also known as "suicide throw"). *Sutemi-nage* takes many forms. The fundamental idea is that, at the moment your opponent commits himself to throw you, you hold on to him and, blending with his momentum, you throw yourself.

When *sutemi-nage* is properly executed, the effect is decisive. All your opponent's power, multiplied by your weight times velocity, is turned against him. Just when victory was in his grasp he finds himself stunned, smashed onto the mat.

Aikido takes the strategy of yielding even further, making it an integral part of every technique. Aikidoists train to draw the attack they want and then to "blend" with it. A skilled aikidoist gives an attacker the illusion that a punch or kick will actually land. Then, applying graceful circular and spiral movements, he redirects the force of the blow, luring the opponent into a helpless position.

One of boxing's greatest upsets provides a marvelous example of the strategy of "yielding to destroy." In 1974, Muhammad Ali defeated George Foreman in the classic "Rumble in the Jungle" by "yielding" to Foreman's superior firepower. In this epic battle, Ali lay against the ropes, covering up for seven rounds, as Foreman pounded away. Ali proved himself a master at "rolling with the punches," and his sacrifice paid off: he knocked the exhausted Foreman out in round eight. Having reclaimed the world title, Ali christened this masterpiece of strategy "The Rope-a-Dope."

In chess, the art of sacrifice is a critical aspect of the Grandmaster's strategic arsenal.

When the enemy comes running to strike you, step aside, avoid him. Immediately attack and cut him down.

—Morihei Ueshiba

BOBBY FISCHER—THE SHOGUN OF SACRIFICE

Bobby Fischer, the brash, unschooled Brooklyn teenager who toppled the might of the Soviet chess system before his thirtieth birthday, is the only American World Champion and the only non-Soviet or non-Russian title-holder since World War II.

In many ways Fischer's story epitomizes the self-reliant, frontier ideals of modern America. (It also provided the inspiration for *Chess*, the Tim Rice/Abba musical.) Yet the dream evaporated after Fischer took the World Championship from Boris Spassky in 1972. Inexplicably, Fischer renounced chess totally and did not play a single competitive game for twenty years. He did not even visit a chess club or chess event as a spectator until his return match with Spassky in September 1992.

Fischer's World Championship match with Spassky was characterized by his detailed demands and his near refusal to play. Once Fischer had condescended to play, however, events took a miraculous course. He began to play magnificent chess, which he backed up with an extraordinary battery of psychological pressures, protesting about both the playing conditions and the board. The Russians retaliated by having the hall swept for electronic and chemical equipment and X-raying the players' chairs. The match ended in a crushing victory for Fischer, but it had strangely traumatic effects on both players. Spassky subsequently disappeared into a shell of caution, Fischer into self-imposed exile, like that of Paul Morphy, the earlier American genius. Yet Fischer's demands performed one lasting service to the followers of chess and to his fellow professionals. The vast size of modern prize funds is a direct result of his insistence that chess players should be paid on a scale comparable with champions in other sports. And his cult of invincibility created a massive upsurge in the popularity of chess.

White: Bobby Fischer; Black: Boris Spassky
World Championship, Reykjavik 1972
Queen's Gambit Declined

This game, the sixth in the most famous World Championship match ever played, was instrumental in deciding the outcome. Widely regarded as the best game of the match, it is commonly described as the chess equivalent of a Mozart symphony.

1	c4	e6
2	♘f3	d5
3	d4	♘f6
4	♘c3	♗e7
5	♗g5	0-0
6	e3	h6
7	♗h4	b6

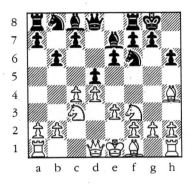

14	♗b5	a6
15	dxc5	bxc5
16	0-0	♖a7
17	♗e2	♘d7
18	♘d4	

The opening, as in Bernstein versus Capablanca, has been a standard Queen's Gambit Declined. White now trades in the center, before Black develops his queen's bishop on b7.

8	cxd5	♘xd5
9	♗xe7	♕xe7
10	♘xd5	exd5
11	♖c1	♗e6

With a black pawn on d5, b7 is no longer a good square for Black's queen's bishop.

12	♕a4	c5

White's next move pins Black's c5-pawn against the black queen.

13	♕a3	♖c8

This is a clever use of the continuing "pin." As we have seen, White's queen on square a3 has pinned Black's pawn on c5, where it shields the queen. Thus immobilized, the pawn is no threat to White's knight on d4. Fischer is playing with wonderful finesse.

18	. . .	♕f8
19	♘xe6	fxe6
20	e4	

This is a beautifully incisive move, which means that Black will have to yield command of at least one diagonal.

Black was threatening to play
. . . c4, offering the trade of
queens and thus activating his
central pawns. Fischer's sacrifice nips this in the bud.

20   . . .   d4

If 20 . . . dxe4 21 ♗c4 ♕e7
22 ♖ce1 ♞f6 23 f3! with a
fierce attack against Black's
broken pawn front.

21	f4	♕e7
22	e5	♖b8
23	♗c4	♔h8
24	♕h3	♞f8
25	b3	a5

After this comes the break-
through on the f-file that enables White to drive a wedge
into the black position.

26	f5	exf5
27	♖xf5	♞h7
28	♖cf1	♕d8
29	♕g3	♖e7
30	h4	♖bb7
31	e6	

Fischer now advances his
passed pawn deep into the
black camp.

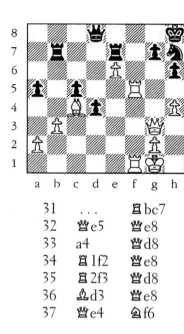

31	. . .	♖bc7
32	♕e5	♕e8
33	a4	♕d8
34	♖1f2	♕e8
35	♖2f3	♕d8
36	♗d3	♕e8
37	♕e4	♞f6

Spassky tries to stem the
flow of White's attack by blocking the f-file with his knight.
However, Fischer brushes this
aside by sacrificing his rook for
the black knight.

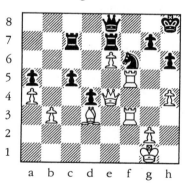

The second sacrifice is now imminent. Without Fischer's inspired next move, giving up rook for knight, White could not break through. It is impressive in this game to see how Fischer is constantly prepared to sacrifice material at critical moments in exchange for strategic momentum or tactical advantages.

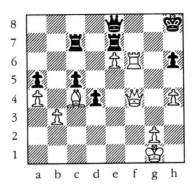

38	♖xf6	gxf6
39	♖xf6	♔g8
40	♗c4	♔h8
41	♕f4	

Here Black resigned the game. The only means of averting ♖f8+ would have been 41 . . . ♔g8, to which Fischer would have replied 42 ♕xh6, which annihilates all the protection around the black king.

Good memory, concentration, and a very strong will.

—Bobby Fischer, on the qualities of a great chess player

20

THE SEAMLESS WEB

The concept of offense and defense lies in adapting each of one's actions to one's enemy, much in the way a sailor will raise the sail when the wind rises, or a hunter will release the hawk on sighting the rabbit. It is usual to think of offense purely in terms of offense and defense purely in terms of defense: however, there are elements of defense in offense and offense in defense.

—Kami-Izumi-Ise no Kami (b. 1508),
founder of the Shinkagi *ryu*

Whatever their individual styles, the greatest players weave all seven strands of Samurai strategy into a seamless web. They understand that the best defense is a good offense and that the best offense is predicated on a stifling defense. Champions famous for their brilliant positional play understand that tempo is the key to establishing position, and those renowned for controlling tempo are invariably attuned to nuances of space. Deception, surprise, and sacrifice are the core of every Grandmaster's arsenal, and all the great chess players relish striking the death blow.

Always try to keep your opponent guessing and try to develop a reputation for being strong in either attack or defense. Sun Tzu wrote in *The Art of War:* "An opponent will not know what location to defend against those skilled in attack, while an opponent will also be uncertain as to where to launch his attack against those skilled in defense."

We have chosen the following game between Anatoly Karpov and Garry Kasparov as a supreme example of all the Samurai principles in action and also to pay tribute to the great champions of the present. David Bronstein, the revered chess guru, described the game that brought Kasparov final victory and the supreme title in his 1985 match with Karpov as "outstandingly brilliant—one of the most impressive in the 100 years' history of the championship." The middlegame offensive that Kasparov unleashed was so recondite that to begin with the depth of Black's conception quite baffled the Grandmaster experts in the Moscow pressroom.

This game typified the clash of style of the world's two best players. As the match started, experts characterized Karpov as "essentially repressive" and Kasparov as "basically revolutionary" in their approaches to the solution of chessboard problems. Raymond Keene wrote:

> In Moscow the conflict is currently seen as one of materialism versus sacrifice. Time after time, Kasparov has sacrificed pieces. In game 11 he even parted with his queen, the most powerful piece, to launch a devastating attack. In sharp contrast, Karpov has to entrench himself and absorb the shock attacks.

This brilliant game exhibited all the key Samurai principles that should operate in any well-played game of chess. At the start, as is White's birthright, Karpov flung forward his kingside pawns to launch a dangerous attack. Kasparov met this with an impenetrable wall of defense. Particularly impressive was his use of the black rooks to control White's attacking ambitions from a distance. The doubling of black rooks in the closed e-file was a superb strategic idea, and quite original. Having surmounted Karpov's onslaught, Kasparov himself timed a brilliant sacrificial counterattack perfectly, displaying the art of sacrifice on the kingside to deceive Karpov into believing that the final blow would fall there. At the crucial moment, however, Kasparov surprisingly switched to the other wing. This maneuver won him material, and having once gained the lead he went remorselessly for the knockout, avoiding a couple of desperate last-ditch traps that Karpov set.

White: Anatoly Karpov; Black: Garry Kasparov
World Championship, Moscow 1985
24th, Final and Deciding Game
Sicilian Defense

1	e4	c5

Needing only a draw to clinch the World Championship, Kasparov still selects the sharpest possible defense against White's first move. The score was 12–11 in Kasparov's favor, and this was the last game. A win for Karpov would tie the match, thus leaving Karpov, as the incumbent, still in possession of his title.

2	♘f3	d6
3	d4	cxd4
4	♘xd4	♘f6
5	♘c3	a6
6	♗e2	e6

7	0-0	♗e7
8	f4	0-0

A standard Sicilian Defense. Traditionally, in this line, White's chances lie on the king's flank, Black's, with control of the semi-open c-file, on the opposite wing.

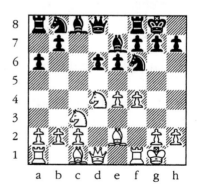

9	♔h1	♛c7
10	a4	♞c6
11	♗e3	♜e8
12	♗f3	♜b8
13	♛d2	♗d7
14	♞b3	b6
15	g4	

16	g5	♞d7
17	♛f2	

Taking the initiative, White attacks.

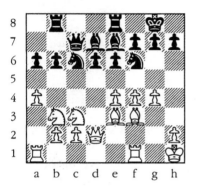

The only disadvantage is that this aggressive pawn move leaves a vacuum in its wake that may represent a future source of weakness.

15   ...   ♗c8

Kasparov retreats an already developed piece, believing he has time to reposition it on the superior square, b7, from where it aims directly at White's king.

White transfers his queen into an attacking position, nearer to the black king. A possible target square for the white queen is h4, bearing down on h7.

17	...	♗f8
18	♗g2	♗b7
19	♜ad1	g6
20	♗c1	♜bc8
21	♜d3	

Introducing a further dangerous attacking scheme. The rook will go to h3.

21	...	♞b4
22	♜h3	♗g7

White hopes to follow up with ♛h4 and f5, but Kasparov has everything under control. White's offensive is hampered by the distance of his knights from the main scene of the action. Still, White should now have struck out with 23 f5!

23	♗e3	♜e7
24	♔g1	♜ce8!

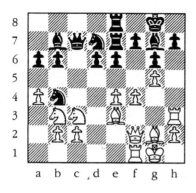

a b c d e f g h

Kasparov's defense is extremely profound and quite impenetrable, culminating in this mysterious doubling-up of his rooks in the closed e-file. The main idea is to discourage White from playing f5, when the answer . . . exf5 will permit Black's rooks to tear down the newly opened central file.

25 ♜d1 f5

Kasparov breaks out and his rooks soon begin to play their part in his counterattack. The text involves an imaginative sacrifice of his b-pawn. This is Black's first sacrifice of the game.

26 gxf6 ♞xf6
27 ♜g3 ♜f7

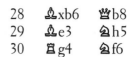

28 ♗xb6 ♕b8
29 ♗e3 ♞h5
30 ♜g4 ♞f6

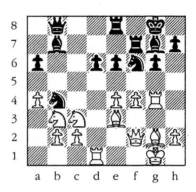

a b c d e f g h

31 ♜h4

The young challenger has timed his counterattack perfectly. In this critical situation, Karpov should now have retreated with 31 ♜g3, but this would have allowed 31 . . . ♞h5 with a draw by repetition of moves, thus giving Kasparov the title. Striving to avoid this sporting calamity, Karpov permits a brilliant new sacrifice. Still, both sides have played excellently, and a draw after 31 ♜g3 would have been a just result.

31 . . . g5!!

Black's second sacrifice: an unexpected blow flinging the remaining chains from Black's forces. In the last few minutes of play, with the World Champion in desperate time trouble, the White position is now utterly routed. Black's 31st is doubly surprising, since Black's counterplay in the Sicilian normally comes on the queen's flank.

32	fxg5	♞g4
33	♕d2	♞xe3
34	♕xe3	♞xc2
35	♕b6	♝a8

This move completes a geometrically elegant retreat, setting up position and distance for the counterattack by . . . ♖b7.

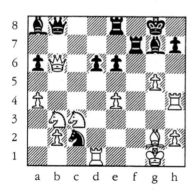

| 36 | ♖xd6 |

This loses a piece. 36 ♕xb8 ♖xb8 37 ♗h3! is the last chance to confuse the issue.

| 36 | . . . | ♖b7 |
| 37 | ♕xa6 | ♖xb3 |

Here 37 . . . ♞b4 would have won more quickly. White's rook on d6 cannot be defended.

| 38 | ♖xe6 | ♖xb2 |
| 39 | ♕c4 | |

Threatening a double mate on e8, which Kasparov sidesteps.

39	. . .	♔h8
40	e5	♕a7+
41	♔h1	♝xg2+

42   ♔xg2
42   ...   ♘d4+

Following through without mercy. White now resigned the game and the title. In the diagram, it was not too late for Kasparov to make a tragic blunder and lose everything after 42 . . . ♖xe6?? 43 ♕c8+ when the "dead lion" would have turned suddenly nasty. This dramatic win made Kasparov, aged twenty-two, the youngest World Champion in the history of chess.

21

TEST YOUR STRENGTH

How good a player are you now? We give you a chance to find out through a sequence of ranking puzzles. You have the opportunity to test yourself in positions from top players' games and discover how your skill compares. Each of the seven Samurai principles is illustrated by two puzzles. Answers are on pages 232 through 233.

As we know, chess is like the martial arts, in that serious players are graded according to their known ability. Martial artists have their *kyu* and *dan* ranks, chess players have Elo ratings. At the end of the series you should have a rough idea of the kind of score you might achieve and where you stand in the competitive world of chess. The table on pages 39 through 40 enables you to assess your rating against the benchmark playing levels.

The positions are all from games involving top Grandmasters and world title challengers such as Nigel Short, Viswanathan Anand, Jan Timman, and Gata Kamsky, or World Champions such as Kasparov and Karpov. Indeed, every player who has competed since the late 1980s in a World Championship match final (whether of the World Chess Federation or of the Professional Chess Association) is represented in these fourteen puzzles.

Keep a record of the time you take for each one. For each position solved in less than two minutes, award yourself ten points; in less than four minutes, five points; in less than six minutes, one point. At the end, total your score, and turn it into an Elo rating.

140 points or more – 2000 strength player – Black belt level
70 points or more – 1600 strength player – Brown belt level
14 points or more – 1400 strength player – Upper green belt level

If you solve at least half the puzzles correctly, but take more than six minutes per puzzle, you can consider yourself a 1200 strength player, standard green belt.

THE FIRST SAMURAI PRINCIPLE—
TAKE THE INITIATIVE: ATTACK

1. From Kasparov v. Bareev, Tilburg 1991. How did the World Champion, White to play, force either a decisive gain of material or checkmate in just a few moves?

White to move and win

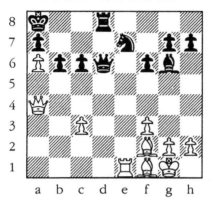

2. This is a variation from Short v. Seirawan, Rotterdam 1989. White is a pawn up, but the most important feature of the position is his pressure against the black queen's wing. How does he land a killer blow?

White to move and win

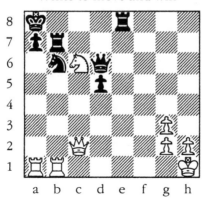

The second Samurai principle—
Follow through: Go for the knockout

3. This position is a possible finish from the game Short v. Kamsky at Tilburg in 1991. White has given up a piece but has a powerful lineup on the d-file. How does he make the most of this?

White to move and win

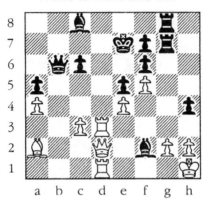

4. This is a possible conclusion from Short v. Adams, London, 1991. The clash between England's two hottest prospects resulted in a win for the more experienced Short. How did he intend to finish off here?

White to move and win

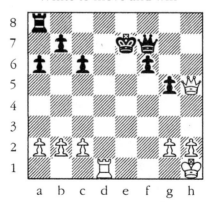

The third Samurai principle—
Impenetrable defense: No openings

5. From Short v. Speelman, London 1991. White now has a chance to capture the black queen. Should he take the bait?

White to move and win

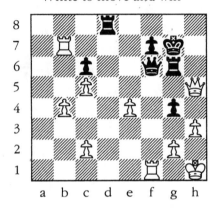

6. From Anand v. Kasparov, World Championship, New York 1995. Black is desperate, but he has one threat. How should White play?

White to move and win

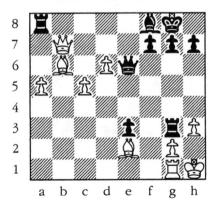

THE FOURTH SAMURAI PRINCIPLE—
TIMING: CONTROL THE TEMPO

7. In 1992 Kasparov scored a most remarkable result when he beat the German Olympiad team, composed entirely of players of Grandmaster strength, contesting all the games simultaneously. This is from his game against Wahls. How does White win?

White to move and win

8. From Kasparov v. Ivanchuk, Moscow 1988. If White does not strike promptly, Black's pieces will reorganize themselves so that Black can escape from his difficulties. What should he do?

White to move and win

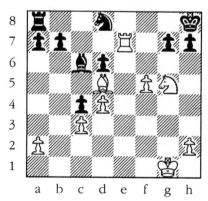

The fifth Samurai principle—
Distance: Control the position

9. From Short v. Timman, Tilburg 1991. The white king has inadvertently wandered up the board. How did White make the most of his mobile monarch?

White to move and win

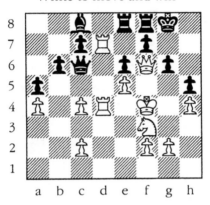

10. From Anand v. Kasparov, World Championship, New York 1995. White can win a pawn with 1 ♖xh4. Should he?

White to move and win

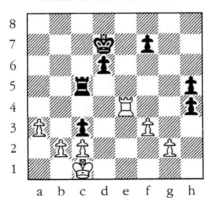

THE SIXTH SAMURAI PRINCIPLE— MASTER SURPRISE AND DECEPTION

11. Variation from Karpov v. Kasparov, World Championship, New York 1990. Black's queen pins White's knight, but Karpov has a surprise in store. The knight is a decoy!

White to move and win

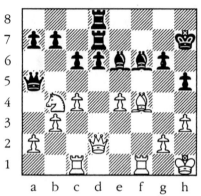

12. From Kasparov v. Timman, Tilburg 1991, one of Kasparov's numerous wins against one of the 1993 FIDE World Championship finalists. How did White force an immediate win on material?

White to move and win

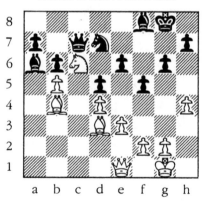

THE SEVENTH SAMURAI PRINCIPLE—
YIELD TO WIN: THE ART OF SACRIFICE

13. From Kasparov v. Larsen, Brussels 1987. Many of White's pieces are pointing dangerously at the black king. How did the World Champion conclude the game with a brilliant sacrifice?

White to move and win

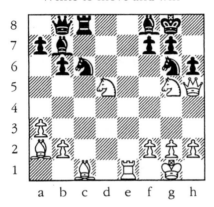

14. From Anand v. Kasparov, World Championship, New York 1995. White is a pawn up, but his king is displaced and his pieces scattered. How does Black shatter the mold?

Black to move and win

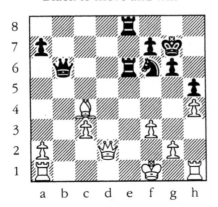

ANSWERS TO RANKING PUZZLES

1.   1 ♖xe7 ♕xe7 2 ♕xc6+ ♚b8 3 ♗g3+.

2.   1 ♖xb6 wins (1 . . . ♖xb6 2 ♖xa7 checkmate).

3.   White bulldozes through with 1 ♖d7+ ♗xd7 2 ♕xd7+ ♚f8 3 ♕c8+, with mate to follow.

4.   1 ♖d7+ wins the black queen.

5.   Certainly not! After 1 ♖xf6 ♖d1+ 2 ♚h2 g3 would be mate. White actually played 1 ♖xf7+ and won easily.

6.   Black's threat is . . . ♖xh3+, but 1 ♚h2!! puts paid to all Black's threats, e.g., 1 . . . ♕e5 2 ♕xa8 and there is no useful discovered check by the black rook.

7.   White finishes with a classic smothered mate: 1 ♘f7+ ♚g8 (1 . . . ♖xf7 2 ♕d8+, with mate to follow) 2 ♘h6++ ♚h8 3 ♕g8+ ♖xg8 4 ♘f7 mate.

8.   Despite the reduced material, White signaled a mating attack with 1 f6 ♗xd5 (1 . . . gxf6 2 ♖xh7 mate) 2 ♖e8+ ♗g8 3 f7 and mate next move.

9.   White ignores the attack on his rook and marches on with 1 ♚g5 ♗xd7 2 ♚h6, and ♕g7 checkmate follows.

10. He did succumb to temptation, but it's wrong. Black then split White's pawns with 1 . . . cxb2+ and drew. Correct is 1 b4!! creating two connected passed pawns.

11. 1 ♘d5 wins, e.g., 1 . . . cxd5 2 ♕xa5, or 1 . . . ♕xd2 2 ♘xf6+ ♚g7 3 ♗xd2 with an extra piece. White's first move is so shocking, because it exposes two white pieces, knight and queen, to black attack.

12. With 1 ♕c1 White sets up the killing double threat of 2 bxa6 and 2 ♘e7+. 1 ♕c3 is equally valid.

13. White won with 1 ♕xg6 as if 1 . . . fxg6, then 2 ♘e7++ ♚h8 3 ♘xg6 mate and if 1 . . . hxg5 2 ♘f6+ ♚h8 3 ♕h7 mate.

14. 1 . . . ♘e4! If the knight is taken with 26 fxe4 then 26 . . .
     ♖f6+ 27 ♔e1 ♖xe4+ 28 ♗e2 ♕f2+ 29 ♔d1 ♖xe2 30
     ♕xe2 ♖d6+. Alternatively, if White spurns Black's offer
     with 26 ♕e1 then 26 . . . ♖d6 27 ♖d1 ♖xd1 28 ♕xd1 al-
     lows a choice of mates with 28 . . . ♕f2 or 28 . . . ♘g3.

Now add up your points and check your strength!

CONCLUSION

The time has come to summarize (or even "samurize") our most important conclusions.

Martial arts and mental sports represent refinements of the human urge to fight and destroy. Mental sports, such as chess and go, simulate war. Many leading military figures—Napoleon, George Washington, Ivan the Terrible, Peter the Great, and, in our own time, Russia's General Lebed and Israeli Defense Minister Anatoly Sharansky—have been avid players. (Sharansky even beat Kasparov in a simultaneous game in 1996.)

Mental sports also represent a sublimation of the aggressive instinct. No blood is spilled, no bones are broken, no body counts are necessary. However, ego, self-delusion, and pride are frequent casualties. Although they are undoubtedly a powerful tool for training minds to make war effectively, mental sports have even greater potential to train minds that can thrive in peacetime, especially at a time in history, such as our own, when "intellectual capital" is at a premium.

Most modern martial arts, and certainly those derived from the Samurai tradition, began as systems for efficient killing. Nevertheless, the greatest masters—Musashi, Tesshu, Kano, Funakoshi, and Ueshiba—all ultimately emphasized the life-affirming, character-building, spiritually edifying aspects of their arts.

In *Samurai Chess* we have brought together these two compelling metaphors, because life is a game, and we want you to play well. In an increasingly complex, rapidly changing world, success in the game requires mastering the art of strategy. The essential purpose of *Samurai Chess*, beyond dramatically improving your chess game, is to develop your talent as a strategic thinker. The Japanese word for strategy is *heiho*. Although modern literature and film refer to the "Samurai swordsman," the original name was *heihōjin*: "strategist."

Strategists seek truth, searching for central principles that can be applied to any situation. Our goal in *Samurai Chess* is to deepen your appreciation of these central principles so that you will, in Musashi's words, "see the Way in everything."

The effective application of these principles depends on knowing yourself and your enemy—and ensuring that they are not one and the same!—and on a commitment to prepare and practice with discipline and passion. The superior strategist cultivates a winning attitude based on learning from mistakes, and knows that physical stamina, strength, flexibility, and poise are critical elements in achieving high performance in any discipline.

We remind you of the Seven Samurai principles, set out in Part Four:

- Take the initiative: Attack
- Follow through: Go for the knockout
- Impenetrable defense: No openings
- Timing: Control the tempo
- Distance: Control the position
- Master surprise and deception
- Yield to win: The art of sacrifice

These offer a guide to success in chess, business, and life. To quote Musashi, "you must research this deeply."

GLOSSARY

MARTIAL ARTS

Aikido A powerful martial art employing spiral movement to redirect attacking force: "the way of harmonious spirit" — *ai* (harmony), *ki* (spirit), *do* (way to enlightenment).
Atemi-waza Striking techniques.
Bokken Wooden sword.
Budo Japanese tradition of cultivating martial prowess, mental and spiritual development, and social responsibility.
Bu-jitsu The practical techniques of fighting.
Bushido "The way of the warrior" — codified during the reign of the Tokugawa *shoguns* beginning in 1603.
Dan Black belt rank.
De-ai Timing, the moment of truth.
Dojo Training center, "place for the refinement of spirit."
Hara The physical center of gravity: "Guts!"
Irimi Entering through an opponent's center.
Jeet kune do Bruce Lee's synthesis of wing chun, kung fu, and modern martial science.
Kami shitoe Japanese expression suggesting that attention to the

tiniest detail can mean the difference between life and death. (The character signifying life is printed on one side of a piece of paper, the character signifying death on the other.)

Karate Devastatingly effective fighting system originated in Okinawa in response to the banning of weapons (literally— "empty hands").

Kendo "The way of the sword."

Ki "Current" of vital power, known as *chi* in China, *prana* in India, and "the Force" in *Star Wars*.

Kiai Concentrated projection of *ki*, often manifested through a shout.

Kohei Junior student.

Kyu Grading levels before black belt.

Ma-ai The appropriate distance between you and your opponent.

Randori Multiple-person attack (the martial equivalent of a simultaneous display).

Reigi Etiquette.

Ryu Family or clan passing down a martial tradition—for instance, Uechi-ryu karate.

Samurai From the verb *samuru*, meaning to serve or protect.

Seiza Sitting posture of the Samurai.

Sempai Senior student.

Sensei Teacher, master (literally "one who comes before").

Seppuku Ritual suicide by disembowelment.

Shihan Professor, Grandmaster, model teacher.

Shodan First-degree black belt (literally, "first step").

Tenkan Turning to seek an advantage.

Waza Technique.

Zanshin Continuing mind, unbroken concentration.

CHESS

Bishop A medium-strength piece (minor piece), equal to the knight, but less valuable than the queen or rook. Moves diagonally only.

Castling A special move to centralize a rook and bring the king into safety.

Check A threat administered by a piece of one side to the opposing king.

Checkmate The termination of the game, usually abbreviated to "mate." When one player is faced by a check that he cannot parry, he is said to be checkmated and has therefore lost the game.

Chessboard The field of battle: a board of 64 squares (8x8) alternating black and white. A white square is always at the right-hand side of each player as he or she faces the board.

Chess clock Clock used to time a player's moves in serious tournament play and lightning (blitz) games.

Combination A forcing sequence of moves with an advantageous goal in view, normally involving a sacrifice of material.

Correspondence chess Chess played by post.

Discovered attack An attack brought about by a moving piece unleashing the full force of a friendly piece aligned behind it.

Doubled pawn Two pawns of the same color on the same file.

Draw Recognition by both players that neither can achieve victory. If the players agree to a draw, each receives half a point. There are several ways of reaching a draw: by mutual agreement, stalemate, repetition of position, or by the 50-move rule.

En passant A special rule allowing a pawn capture on an empty square in certain situations.

Equality A state of equilibrium between the two sides. An "equal" position offers balanced chances to both White and Black.

Exchange To gain (or lose) the "exchange" means to gain or lose a rook for a minor piece (bishop or knight).

Fork A simultaneous attack against two or more pieces.

Gambit A sacrifice of one or more pawns early in the game to further rapid development of the pieces or to gain tempi (tempo = time unit).

Isolated pawn A pawn with no allied pawns on either file adjacent to it.

King The most important piece. In the middlegame it should shelter behind pawns, while in the endgame it may emerge when its value is equivalent to approximately a bishop or a knight. Attack on the king is known as check, and a check that cannot be parried is checkmate, thus ending the game.

Knight A minor piece, equivalent to a bishop. It is the only piece that can standardly leap over obstacles friendly or hostile. The knight always ends on a square of opposite color to that on which it began the move.

Mate See checkmate.

Notational systems Systems for recording chess moves. The currently used system is Simplified Modern Notation. In its shortened form this specifies only the square on which a piece lands, not the one from which it moves.

Open file A file completely empty of pawns of each color.

Pawn The foot soldier of chess. Can only advance, and may never retreat. On reaching the eighth rank can be promoted to rook, bishop, knight, or queen, queen being the usual choice.

Pin A pin arises when an attacked piece shields a friendly unit of even greater value. Any piece that is pinned to the king cannot move at all.

Problem Composed exercises with a given task in view—in contrast with positions in games arising from over-the-board play.

Promotion Promotion only occurs when a pawn reaches the eighth rank (see pawn).

Queen The most powerful, though not the most important, piece. The queen is worth approximately three minor pieces or two rooks, and moves both diagonally and in straight lines.

Rook Second in value only to the queen. Moves exclusively in straight lines.

Sacrifice A surrender of material to gain compensating advantages in an alternative form, such as the initiative, an attack, superior mobility.

Scoresheet A sheet of paper used during match play on which chess games are recorded.

Skewer An attack against a piece that forces the capture of another hostile unit farther down the line of fire.

Stalemate Stalemate is a draw and occurs when one side, without being in checkmate, has completely run out of legal moves.

Study See Problem.

Underpromotion Promotion by a pawn to rook, knight, or bishop rather than queen.

FURTHER READING
AND INFORMATION

Gichin Funakoshi, *Karate-do: My Way of Life*, New York and London: Kodansha International, 1975. The autobiography of the founder of Shotokan karate.

Michael Gelb, *Body Learning: An Introduction to the Alexander Technique*, London: Aurum Press, 1981, new edition, 1995; New York: Henry Holt, 1987 and 1995. *Publishers Weekly* called this the most lucid book on the subject.

Michael Gelb and Tony Buzan, *Lessons from the Art of Juggling: How to Achieve Your Full Potential in Business, Learning and Life*, London: Aurum Press, 1994; New York: Harmony Books, 1994. More fun with metaphor.

Michael Gelb, *Thinking For A Change: Discovering the Power to Create, Communicate and Lead*, London: Aurum Press, 1996; Harmony Books: New York, 1996. Strategies for success in a changing world.

Eugen Herrigel, *Zen in the Art of Archery*, New York: Vintage Books, 1971. The original Zen application book, offering penetrating insights into attaining excellence in any discipline.

Raymond Keene and Garry Kasparov, *Batsford Chess Openings 2*, London: Batsford, 1989; New York: Henry Holt, 1989. The standard one-volume chess encyclopedia, which has sold over 100,000 copies.

Raymond Keene, *The Times Winning Moves II*, London: Batsford, 1996; New York: Henry Holt, 1996. Selection of fascinating puzzles from Ray Keene's daily chess column in *The Times*.

Raymond Keene and David Levy, *How to Beat your Chess Computer*, London: Batsford, 1991; New York: Henry Holt, 1991. Tailor-made strategies to defeat the silicon monsters.

Lao-tsu, *Tao Te Ching: A New English Version*, with Foreword and Notes by Stephen Mitchell, New York: Harper and Row, 1988. A masterpiece of synvergent thinking.

Bruce Lee, *Tao of Jeet Kune Do*, Santa Clarita, CA: Ohara Publications, 1975. The martial journal of a genius.

Frederick Lovret, *The Way and the Power: Secrets of Japanese Strategy*, Boulder: Paladin Press, 1987. Lovret's approach may seem rather severe, but if you were in a fight you would definitely want him on your side.

Miyamoto Musashi, *A Book of Five Rings*, translated by Victor Harris, London: Allison and Busby, 1974; Woodstock, NY: Overlook Press, 1974. The classic of martial arts strategy.

Aron Nimzowitsch, *My System—Classic Chess Strategy*, London: Batsford, 1995; Dallas: Hayes Publishing, 1992. Written in the 1920s, this book remains the Bible of strategic thinking in chess.

Mitsugi Saotome, *Aikido and the Harmony of Nature*, Boston and London: Shambhala, 1993. Saotome sensei was a live-in student of Morihei Ueshiba for fifteen years and has been training in aikido for almost half a century.

John Stevens, *Abundant Peace: The Biography of Morihei Ueshiba*, Boston and London: Shambhala, 1987. The fascinating story of aikido's founder.

John Stevens, *The Sword of No-Sword: The Biography of Yamaoku Tesshu*, Boulder and London: 1984; Shambhala, 1984. Stevens brings sword-master Tesshu to life.

Sun Tzu, *The Art of War*, London and New York: Oxford University Press, 1963. The masterpiece of strategy.

Kisshomaru Ueshiba, *The Spirit of Aikido*, New York and London: Kodansha International, 1984. The son of the founder communicates aikido's spiritual essence.

Internet site

Ray Keene's daily chess column, giving the latest chess news and top games, can be accessed via *The Times* at the following site: http://www.the-times.co.uk

Further Information

To learn more about the ideas and methods of Samurai Chess, you may wish to inquire about "The Creative Strategy Seminar" with Michael Gelb and Grandmaster Raymond Keene. This unforgettable two-day program includes an introduction to the game of chess, participation in a simultaneous chess display against Grandmaster Raymond Keene, an aikido demonstration and class, and an introduction to mind-mapping. Participants are then guided to apply these metaphors and tools of strategic thinking to solving their most important business problems. Contact: **Michael Gelb, President, High Performance Learning®, 9844 Beach Mill Road, Great Falls, Virginia 22066, USA (tel: 703-757-7007, fax: 703-757-7211), email: GelbThink@aol.com, or Grandmaster Raymond Keene OBE, 86 Clapham Common North Side, London SW4 9SE, United Kingdom (tel: 0171-228-7009, fax: 0171-924-6472).**

The High Performance Learning Center® (HPL) is an international leadership training and consulting firm founded by Michael J. Gelb in 1982. HPL guides individuals and organizations to define and realize their highest aspirations. HPL helps leaders to "walk their talk"—to build teamwork, creativity, communication, trust, and organizational alignment. A catalyst for creative change, HPL bridges the gap between visions of exceptional quality, superior service and personal fulfillment, and everyday behavior. HPL's programs are all customized to achieve specific client goals. HPL also supplies a wide range of resources designed to support and extend the work carried out with individuals and in small groups.

If you want to join a chess club or need more information about any aspect of chess, contact: The British Chess Federation, 9a Grand Parade, St. Leonards-on-Sea, East Sussex TN38 ODD, UK (tel: 01424-442500, fax: 01424-718372) or the United States Chess Federation, 186 Route 9W, New Windsor, NY 12550, USA (tel: 914-562-8350, fax: 914-561-2437).

Information on teachers of the Alexander Technique can be obtained from The Society of Teachers of the Alexander Technique (STAT), 20 London House, 266 Fulham Road, London SW10 9EL (tel: 0171-351-0828, fax: 0171-352-1556) or The North America Society of Teachers of the Alexander Technique (NASTAT), PO Box 112484, Tacoma, WA 98411-2484 (tel: 206-627-3766).

A listing of aikido schools worldwide can be obtained from *Aikido Today* magazine, Arete Press, P.O. Box 1060, Claremont, Ca. 91711 (tel: 909-624-7770, fax: 909-398-1840).

INDEX

Women, 12–14
Woolley, Sir Leonard, 15
World Chess Champions, 19, 20,
    193, 222, 223
    killer instinct, 94
World Chess Championship, 26, 152,
    200, 206, 211
    dominated by USSR/Russia, 22
    1986, 23–24
    1995, 124
    purse for, 27
World Championship matches,
    107–8, 194, 212, 223
    gamesmanship in, 142–43

Moscow, 1966, 88
    preparation for, 156–57
    Spassky v. Fischer, 141
World Chess Federation (FIDE), 39,
    223

Yield to win, 173, 210–15, 231, 235

Zanshin ("continuing mind"),
    181–86
Zen, 31–32, 34
Zen and the Art of Archery (Herrigel),
    156
Zugzwang syndrome, 191

ABOUT THE AUTHORS

Michael J. Gelb has an international reputation as a pioneer in the fields of creative thinking, mind/body coordination, and leadership development. Many organizations seek out his services as a strategic adviser. Michael Gelb created the Juggling Metaphor Method and, with Tony Buzan, wrote *Lessons From the Art of Juggling*. He also introduced the concept of synvergent thinking in his book *Thinking for a Change*. Michael's book *Body Learning: An Introduction to the Alexander Technique* has been translated into eleven languages. A student of the martial arts since 1968, Michael Gelb has studied karate, kung fu, tai chi chuan, boxing, and wrestling. He holds a *sandan* (third-degree black belt) in aikido with certification as an instructor by Dr. Clyde Takeguchi of the United States Aikido Federation. In 1995 Michael Gelb founded "Global Aikido," a mobile *dojo* specializing in guiding organizations and individuals to apply the principles of aikido to daily life. An avid student of mind sports, Michael Gelb is approaching *shodan* (black belt) level in go, and prides himself on having once achieved a draw game of chess with Raymond Keene.

Raymond Keene is the world's leading authority on chess and

mind sports. An International Chess Grandmaster since 1976 and ex–Bristish Champion, Keene is author of ninety-seven books. He writes a daily chess column in *The Times* and a weekly one in *The Sunday Times*. A primary organizer of the World Chess Championship Match between Garry Kasparov and Nigel Short and cofounder of the International Mind Sports Olympiad, Raymond was awarded an OBE (Officer of the British Empire) by Her Majesty Queen Elizabeth in 1985. A graduate of Cambridge University, Keene is fluent in German, Spanish, and French. He is a lively presenter with over five hundred TV appearances worldwide. An enthusiastic student of martial arts, Raymond recently was awarded his sixth *Kyu* certificate in aikido.